W9-AGH-931

Divorce

Other Books of Related Interest:

Opposing Viewpoints Series

American Values

Domestic Violence

Family

At Issue Series

Polygamy

Current Controversies Series

Family Violence

Violence Against Women

"Congress shall make no law . . . abridging the freedom of speech, or of the press."

First Amendment to the U.S. Constitution

The basic foundation of our democracy is the First Amendment guarantee of freedom of expression. The Opposing Viewpoints Series is dedicated to the concept of this basic freedom and the idea that it is more important to practice it than to enshrine it.

Divorce

Mike Wilson, Book Editor

GREENHAVEN PRESS
A part of Gale, Cengage Learning

Detroit • New York • San Francisco • New Haven, Conn • Waterville, Maine • London

Christine Nasso, *Publisher*
Elizabeth Des Chenes, *Managing Editor*

For more information, contact:
Greenhaven Press
27500 Drake Rd.
Farmington Hills, MI 48331-3535
Or you can visit our Internet site at gale.cengage.com

Articles in Greenhaven Press anthologies are often edited for length to meet page requirements. In addition, original titles of these works are changed to clearly present the main thesis and to explicitly indicate the author's opinion. Every effort is made to ensure that Greenhaven Press accurately reflects the original intent of the authors. Every effort has been made to trace the owners of copyrighted material.

Cover photograph reproduced by permission of Mike Kemp/Rubberball Productions/Getty Images.

LIBRARY OF CONGRESS CATALOGING-IN-PUBLICATION DATA

Divorce / Mike Wilson, book editor.
p. cm. -- (Opposing viewpoints)
Includes bibliographical references and index.
ISBN-13: 978-0-7377-4204-6 (hardcover)
ISBN-13: 978-0-7377-4205-3 (pbk.)
1. Divorce. I. Wilson, Mike, 1954-
HQ814.D586 2008
306.89--dc22

2008032031

Printed in the United States of America
1 2 3 4 5 6 7 12 11 10 09 08

Contents

Why Consider Opposing Viewpoints?

> *"The only way in which a human being can make some approach to knowing the whole of a subject is by hearing what can be said about it by persons of every variety of opinion and studying all modes in which it can be looked at by every character of mind. No wise man ever acquired his wisdom in any mode but this."*
>
> *John Stuart Mill*

In our media-intensive culture it is not difficult to find differing opinions. Thousands of newspapers and magazines and dozens of radio and television talk shows resound with differing points of view. The difficulty lies in deciding which opinion to agree with and which "experts" seem the most credible. The more inundated we become with differing opinions and claims, the more essential it is to hone critical reading and thinking skills to evaluate these ideas. Opposing Viewpoints books address this problem directly by presenting stimulating debates that can be used to enhance and teach these skills. The varied opinions contained in each book examine many different aspects of a single issue. While examining these conveniently edited opposing views, readers can develop critical thinking skills such as the ability to compare and contrast authors' credibility, facts, argumentation styles, use of persuasive techniques, and other stylistic tools. In short, the Opposing Viewpoints Series is an ideal way to attain the higher-level thinking and reading skills so essential in a culture of diverse and contradictory opinions.

In addition to providing a tool for critical thinking, Opposing Viewpoints books challenge readers to question their own strongly held opinions and assumptions. Most people form their opinions on the basis of upbringing, peer pressure, and personal, cultural, or professional bias. By reading carefully balanced opposing views, readers must directly confront new ideas as well as the opinions of those with whom they disagree. This is not to simplistically argue that everyone who reads opposing views will—or should—change his or her opinion. Instead, the series enhances readers' understanding of their own views by encouraging confrontation with opposing ideas. Careful examination of others' views can lead to the readers' understanding of the logical inconsistencies in their own opinions, perspective on why they hold an opinion, and the consideration of the possibility that their opinion requires further evaluation.

Evaluating Other Opinions

To ensure that this type of examination occurs, Opposing Viewpoints books present all types of opinions. Prominent spokespeople on different sides of each issue as well as well-known professionals from many disciplines challenge the reader. An additional goal of the series is to provide a forum for other, less known, or even unpopular viewpoints. The opinion of an ordinary person who has had to make the decision to cut off life support from a terminally ill relative, for example, may be just as valuable and provide just as much insight as a medical ethicist's professional opinion. The editors have two additional purposes in including these less known views. One, the editors encourage readers to respect others' opinions—even when not enhanced by professional credibility. It is only by reading or listening to and objectively evaluating others' ideas that one can determine whether they are worthy of consideration. Two, the inclusion of such viewpoints encourages the important critical thinking skill of objectively evaluating an author's credentials and bias. This evaluation will illuminate an author's reasons for taking a particular stance on an issue and will aid in readers' evaluation of the author's ideas.

It is our hope that these books will give readers a deeper understanding of the issues debated and an appreciation of the complexity of even seemingly simple issues when good and honest people disagree. This awareness is particularly important in a democratic society such as ours in which people enter into public debate to determine the common good. Those with whom one disagrees should not be regarded as enemies but rather as people whose views deserve careful examination and may shed light on one's own.

Thomas Jefferson once said that "difference of opinion leads to inquiry, and inquiry to truth." Jefferson, a broadly educated man, argued that "if a nation expects to be ignorant and free . . . it expects what never was and never will be." As individuals and as a nation, it is imperative that we consider the opinions of others and examine them with skill and discernment. The Opposing Viewpoints Series is intended to help readers achieve this goal.

David L. Bender and Bruno Leone,
Founders

Introduction

> *"Every society requires a critical mass of families that fit the traditional ideal, both to meet the needs of most children and to serve as a model for other adults who are raising children in difficult settings. We are at risk of losing that critical mass in America today."*
>
> *Hillary R. Clinton,*
> *It Takes a Village*

Divorce is something that affects most Americans directly or indirectly. According to a 2006 Gallup poll, 30 percent of adult Americans say they have been divorced at some point in their lifetimes, up from 23 percent in 1985. Nearly everyone either has been divorced or has family members or close friends who have been divorced. Many married couples who do not divorce have nonetheless thought about it. Among those who are married, a 2008 Roper Poll found that 33 percent have at some point considered divorce. Women were more likely than men (39 percent vs. 27 percent) to have at least thought about divorce at some point during their marriage.

Historically, divorce has been both a religious and a civil or secular issue. Some current issues in divorce have antecedents in Judeo-Christian beliefs. Deuteronomy 24:1, customarily attributed to Moses, states that if a man maries a woman "and it comes to pass that she find no favor in his eyes, because he hath found some uncleanness in her; then let him write her a bill of divorcement . . . and send her out of his house." At the time of Jesus, two schools of thought concerning the meaning of Deuteronomy 24:1 existed. One school, led by Rabbi Shammai, argued that the passage meant divorce was permitted only for adultery; the other view, led by Rabbi Hillel, was that a man could divorce his wife for any reason. Analogizing to modern terms, one view required fault as grounds for divorce and the other view permitted the equivalent of a "no-fault" divorce.

The book of Matthew has several statements attributed to Jesus concerning divorce. In Matthew 19:4–6, Jesus states that a man and a woman joined in marriage are "one flesh" and "[t]herefore what God has joined together, let not man separate." A similar passage appears in the book of Mark. When critics challenged Jesus to explain his statement, which appears to contradict Deuteronomy, Jesus states in Matthew 19:8, "Moses, because of the hardness of your hearts, permitted you to divorce your wives, but from the beginning it was not so." In Mark 10:11 and Luke 16:18, Jesus says that those who divorce and remarry commit adultery, which also implies that divorce cannot abolish the marriage bond.

In Matthew 5:32 and 19:9, however, Jesus appears to approve divorce on grounds of adultery. So does Christianity permit divorce or not?

Christianity is divided over divorce. The Catholic Church decreed that marriage is a spiritual sacrament that, once created, remains intact in the eyes of God regardless of the desires or actions of the parties to the marriage. Since true marriage is considered spiritually indissoluble, only annulment of the marriage—a finding that a true marriage never really existed—is permitted. The Eastern Orthodox Church and most Protestant denominations permit divorce if sufficient grounds for divorce exist.

For many centuries in England the ecclesiastical courts, rather than civil courts, regulated dissolution of marriage. The courts only annulled marriages based upon grounds that existed at the time of the marriage. Later people came to regard marriage as a kind of contract, and civil courts began regulating the dissolution of marriages. Divorce was still considered against public policy, but civil courts expanded the grounds for divorce to include conditions that occurred after the marriage if it constituted violation of the marriage vows and if the party requesting the divorce was innocent of any wrongdoing. Circumstances that constituted violation of marriage vows included adultery, abandonment, and extreme cruelty.

The legal system in the United States was based upon that of England, the country of origin for most of the early colonists. Historically, divorce laws in the United States required grounds for granting a divorce. To obtain a divorce, the party had to be without fault. Grounds for divorce varied by state and, prior to the widespread adoption of no-fault divorce, those who could afford to do so would go to Nevada or even outside the United States where they could obtain divorces more easily. Many couples who were not victims of abandonment, adultery, or the like nonetheless wanted to divorce. As a result, many husbands and wives simply fabricated grounds for a divorce and lied under oath.

Divorce reform was proposed by a group assembled by the archbishop of Canterbury based upon the single ground of "irreconcilable differences" without regard to fault. California studied the proposal and adopted the first no-fault divorce law. Today all states except New York have some version of no-fault divorce.

The women's movement also played a role in the development of divorce law, promoting equal distribution of property and better enforcement of child support orders. By the late 1970s, noncustodial fathers began forming groups to fight what they perceived as unfair treatment from divorce courts.

In recent years, various groups have advocated reforms to make divorces more difficult to obtain, suggesting ideas such as a return to fault-based divorce, longer waiting periods, mutual consent for a no-fault divorce, and mandatory counseling and education before marriage and before divorce. Other groups have promoted ideas to "improve" divorce by making it less combative through techniques such as mediation and collaborative divorce. Do-it-yourself divorce kits have become popular in the effort to make divorce less costly.

Americans remain divided over the issue. According to a 2007 Gallup poll, 66 percent of Americans think divorce is morally acceptable, but 26 percent disagree. Notwithstanding religious teachings on the issue of divorce, a 2004 Barna Research poll found that 58 percent of Protestants and 69 percent of Catholics believed that divorce in which the other party had not committed adultery was not a sin. As recently as April 2008, Pope Benedict XVI called divorce a "serious offense" that violates human dignity, inflicts deep injustice on human and social relations, and "offends God himself," yet divorce rates for Catholics exceed 20 percent. A Barna Research survey found that born-again Christians had a higher likelihood of divorce than agnostics and atheists.

Given the very real impact divorce has on people's lives, it is little wonder that so many opposing viewpoints exist. The authors of the following selections examine issues of divorce in chapters focused on four themes: "Is Divorce a Serious Problem?" "Can Divorce Be Prevented?" "Do Divorce Laws Work?" and "Can the Negative Effects of Divorce Be Minimized?" These issues will likely remain a point of controversy well into the future.

Is Divorce a Serious Problem?

Chapter Preface

Is divorce a serious problem? It may depend upon the data examined. While 30 percent of Americans report having gone through a divorce at some point in their lives, Justin Wolfers, a professor at Wharton University, has observed that divorces per one thousand persons has dropped 27 percent since 1979 and is likely to continue declining.

Persons who married during recent decades, however, are less likely to stay married than in the past. The results of the 2004 Census found that about 80 percent of first marriages that took place in the late 1950s lasted at least fifteen years, but among people who married for the first time in the late 1980s, only 61 percent of the men and 57 percent of the women were married fifteen years later.

Those who claim that divorce is a serious problem often point to children as unwilling victims of a divorce. Each year, about 1 million children experience the divorce of their parents—three times the number of children affected by divorce in the 1950s. Senator Hillary R. Clinton, in her book *It Takes a Village*, observed that recent studies demonstrate convincingly that while many adults claim to have benefited from divorce and single parenthood, most children have not. "Children living with one parent or in stepfamilies are two to three times more likely to have emotional and behavioral problems as children living in two-parent families," she argues. "A parent's remarriage often does not seem to better the odds."

Gordon Berlin, executive vice president of MDRC, a social policy research organization, stated in 2004 Congressional testimony that "children who grow up in an intact, two-parent family with both biological parents present do better on a wide range of outcomes than children who grow up in a single-parent family." In addition to difficulties children of divorced parents have growing up, studies show that children of divorced parents are twice as likely to become divorced when they grow up and marry.

But is divorce really to blame for the problems these children experience? A 2002 study by sociologist Yongmin Sun published in the *Journal of Marriage and Family Therapy*, found evidence that problems experienced by children of divorce may not be caused by the divorce itself. Using data from more than ten thousand high school students, Sun compared teens from intact families to teens whose parents would eventually divorce, comparing grades, self-esteem, behavior problems, and substance and alcohol abuse. While those with parents who eventually divorced did more poorly in all areas than those with parents who did not divorce, the teens from divorcing parents did no worse after the divorce than they were doing before the divorce—some even seemed to do better. This suggests that marital conflict that leads to a divorce, rather than divorce itself, is what causes damage to children.

Also, some evidence suggests that most children survive divorce fairly well. According to psychotherapist Samuel M. Portnoy, research shows that two years after divorce 80 percent of children appear to have no major psychological problems, achieve well, and remain close to their families.

As the following viewpoints show, whether divorce is a serious problem and for whom is a hotly debated issue.

Viewpoint 1

> *"Stepcouples face a variety of unique challenges which put them at higher risk for dissolution."*

Stepcouples Are at High Risk for Divorce

Adminstration for Families and Children

The Administration for Families and Children (AFC) argues in the following viewpoint that issues unique to stepcouples make them especially vulnerable to divorce. Parent-child relationships that predate the marriage, a new "instant parent" resulting from remarriage, and the difficulties of co-parenting in separate households all create stress on the stepfamily. Stepcouples, the AFC argues, need realistic expectations about their remarriage and negotiation skills to meet the unique challenges of stepfamilies. AFC is a federal agency that promotes the well-being of families and children.

As you read, consider the following questions:

1. According to the author, how does being a child in a stepfamily, as opposed to a nuclear family, affect the risk of negative outcomes for a child?

Administration for Families and Children, "Stepcouples Are at High Risk for Divorce," U.S. Dept. of Health and Human Services, April 11, 2007.

2. In the author's view, how have marriage education programs addressed relationship complexities of stepfamilies?
3. What stepfamily issues consistently are a key focus of marriage education programs, according to the author?

Stepfamily couples (i.e., "stepcouples") have become common as a result of recent rates of divorces, remarriages, and first marriages following out-of-wedlock births. Stepcouples face a variety of unique challenges which put them at higher risk for dissolution than non-stepfamily couples. These challenges arise in part from complex relationships in the family with stepchildren, former partners, and half- and stepsiblings. Problems stemming from these complexities also put children in stepfamilies at greater risk for negative outcomes than children in nuclear families. Existing marriage education programs do not address these unique stresses for stepfamilies in depth.

While not all stepfamilies have low income, risks for stepcouples are magnified in the context of lower economic resources. Couples experiencing economic strain face additional stresses arising from financial difficulties and other personal and environmental challenges accompanying limited resources. . . .

Unique Characteristics of Stepfamilies

Together our review of research literature on stepfamilies and study of programs yielded a number of observations about stepfamilies and raised questions that future research might address.

From the start, stepfamilies differ from non-stepfamilies in important ways:

- The biological parent-child bond predates the couple's relationship;

- A spouse may become an "instant parent" at marriage rather than having children join the family over time;
- One of the children's biological parents most likely lives in a separate household;
- Children may move between two households;
- The vast majority of stepfamily couples will be navigating at least one co-parenting relationship with a former spouse/partner; and
- Members of the family have experienced the loss of a relationship through separation, divorce, or death.

Marriage educators will be most effective in supporting healthy marriages among stepcouples when this unique family context is considered and addressed in program services. We emphasize that the context is likely to be even more complex and challenging among low-income stepcouples because of the higher incidence of multiple-partner fertility, with its multiple co-parenting relationships, extended family relationships, and sibling relationships. For such families, such complexities can create additional stresses even before adding the difficulties that come with limited financial resources. Because of the complexity of relationships present at the onset of stepcouple formation, marriage education services should utilize an inclusive approach to addressing other relationships in the family system.

Unique Stepfamily Issues Not Recognized

The unique relationship complexities in stepfamilies often are not acknowledged and addressed by stepcouples or marriage education programs. Marriage education programs may not distinguish between stepcouples and nuclear family couples. Few general marriage education programs include program content specific to the stepfamily context.

Stepcouples More Likely to Divorce

Nationally representative data indicate that remarriages (whether children are involved or not) end in divorce at a greater rate than first marriages. It appears that individuals entering remarriage with a child divorce at a higher rate than individuals entering remarriage without children. Dr. [E. Mavis] Hetherington's broader range research sample of both clinical and nonclinical remarriages (though not nationally representative) indicates that over time, the incidence of divorce for couples in remarriages, particularly those with children, may be even greater than previously reported.

Ron Deal, "The Stepcouple Divorce Rate May Be Higher than We Thought," Association of Marriage and Family Ministries, *January 13, 2006. www.amfmonline.com.*

Scholars suggest that the tendency to relegate stepcouples to a "hidden" population owes to societal norms affirming the nuclear family as "ideal." One finds evidence of these norms in the media, fairy tales, and in forms and procedures used by schools and other institutions. Implicit in this treatment are societal pressures for stepcouples to function and develop in the same way as nuclear family couples.

Stepcouples Have Unrealistic Expectations

Many stepcouples enter marriage with the expectation that their marriage will be "just like" marriages where no stepchildren or former partners are involved. The most predominant unrealistic standards include beliefs about functional equivalency to first-marriage families, quick adjustment, and instant love. It is important that stepcouples recognize that their unique family characteristics will have implications for their marital functioning. For example, it often takes a substantial length of time for stepfamily relationships and routines to gel. The first several years are especially likely to be turbulent for stepcouples. Expectations about family bonding, emotional closeness, and love among all of the members of the stepfamily equally may be unrealistic. . . .

Conflicts Between Two Households

Respondents in the [marriage education] program study consistently indicated that tensions between stepparents and stepchildren were a key focus of their programs and that many families sought out support and education because of these issues. Several respondents told us that couples with pre-adolescents and adolescents were especially likely to participate in the programs. This self-selection fits with empirical evidence that stepcouples with pre-adolescent and adolescent children report comparatively more adjustment issues and marital difficulties than stepcouples with younger children.

The marital relationship is affected also by the quality of the co-parenting relationship(s) with former spouses/partners. It is important for stepcouples to be able to keep conflict low when co-parenting and protect the boundaries between households that are necessary for healthy marital functioning.

Although negotiation skills are important for all relationships, stepcouples face added challenges in navigating the roles and norms that are not clearly defined in general societal norms. Financial responsibilities also can be more complicated in stepfamilies, and stepcouples must successfully negotiate a shared vision for their financial practices.

"[When parents divorce] negotiating the difference between the mother's world and the father's world leads to confusion and stress among the children and can have lasting consequences."

Divorce Hurts Children

Michelle Bryant

Michelle Bryant argues in the following viewpoint that divorce harms children in many ways. Children of divorce may lose faith in marriage and become unable to form intimate relationships, she says. Citing research, the author contends that, in most cases, children would be better off if parents with unhappy marriages did not divorce. She argues that divorce creates insecurity and requires children to negotiate between the conflicting worlds of their mothers and fathers. Bryant writes for the University of Texas at Austin's Web site.

As you read, consider the following questions:

1. According to authorities quoted by the author, when do the worst symptoms of the "sleeper effect" from a parent's divorce often appear?

Michelle Bryant, "The Divorce Dilemma: Sociologist Finds that Even Amicable Divorces Are Likely to Have Negative Effects on Children," *The University of Texas at Austin—Feature Story*, March 27, 2006. Reproduced by permission.

2. What fraction of marriages are so bad that it is better for the children if their parents divorce, according to the author?
3. According to the author, children of divorce are how much more likely to be asked by a parent to keep a secret from another parent?

While amicable divorces are certainly better than the alternative, particularly when children are involved, a new national study shows they still take a toll on children's overall well-being, as well as their own future marital success.

Surprisingly, persons whose parents had a good divorce had, on average, the least successful marriages of any of the categories of persons compared. Their results differed significantly from persons whose parents had bad divorces involving destructive behaviors or low-conflict but not happy marriages. Results for that group were considerably poorer than those whose parents had a happy marriage.

"If the parents whose marriage failed are obviously good people who could cooperate and avoid destructive behaviors after the divorce, their offspring may be more inclined to lose confidence in the institution of marriage itself," said Dr. Norval Glenn, sociologist at The University of Texas at Austin and coinvestigator for the study. "Even by being good people and by marrying good people, they feel they cannot assure that their marriage will work."

Glenn, with Elizabeth Marquardt, author of *Between Two Worlds*, codirected the first nationally representative sample survey of 750 children of divorce, ages 18–35 and conducted in-depth interviews with 35 others in the same age range in various parts of the country. For comparative purposes, the researchers also surveyed and did in-depth interviews with an equal number of persons in the same age range whose parents did not divorce. The interview questions were specifically designed to capture the child's perspective. Most previous literature has been written from that of the parents.

Divorce seems to be the most traumatic on those children whose parents were not in a high-conflict marriage. The divorce catches them totally by surprise.

Research in a recent book by Judith Wallerstein, a pioneer in the psychological effects of divorce in children and young people, shows that experiencing parental divorce during childhood has a "sleeper effect." Its worst symptoms often appear when children of divorce leave home and try to form intimate relationships and families of their own, but do so with much less ability to trust and little idea of what a lasting marriage looks like.

"Persons whose parents had extremely bad marriages and bad divorces may be able to blame the failure of their parents' marriage on bad behavior by the parents," Glenn said. "They may not, therefore, lose confidence in the institution of marriage."

He cautions that if there is violence or extreme conflict, or if the marriage is so bad it leaves the primary parent, usually the mother, so depressed she can't parent effectively, the children are usually better off after the parents divorce. However, only a minority of the divorces of couples with children is of this nature—probably no more than about a third. The remainder of the marriages did not clearly have detrimental effects on the well-being or development of the children, and ended because one or both of the spouses felt the marriage was unsatisfactory.

"In most of these cases, the children would almost certainly have benefited from the parents staying together," said Glenn. "These are the cases for which it makes sense to talk about negative consequences of divorce. For persons whose parents had high conflict marriages, it makes sense to talk about negative consequences of failed parental marriages, but the divorces themselves may typically lessen those consequences."

Divorce Creates Permanent Inner Conflict for Children

For those of us from divorced families, a deep and enduring moral drama was ignited the moment our parents parted. After their parting we spent our childhoods crossing a widening chasm as their divided worlds grew more different every year. Our constant journeys between their worlds had lasting consequences.

Most children cannot conceive of keeping important secrets for their parents, but divorce required us to keep secrets routinely, even when our parents did not ask us to. Most children observe their parents confronting each other about their conflicting values and beliefs; sometimes these confrontations end in fights, sometimes in agreement, sometimes in stalemate. But the majority of those from divorced families say that as the years passed, our divorced parents did *not* have a lot of conflicts. Instead, we experienced something much deeper and more pernicious. The divorce left us with a permanent inner conflict between our parents' worlds. This was a conflict for which we could imagine no resolution, a conflict for which many of us thought we had only ourselves to blame.

Elizabeth Marquardt,
Between Two Worlds: The Inner Lives of Children of Divorce.
New York: Crown Books, 2005.

"Good divorce," a term introduced by Constance Ahrons's influential 1994 book titled *The Good Divorce*, typically is used to describe the amicable divorce that avoids pitfalls such as involving children in parental conflict. It has been thought to prevent or substantially lessen the negative consequences on children, supporting the notion that divorce itself is less important than the way parents handle it. However, this is not quite correct in terms of the effects on children. While divorces that end highly destructive marriages are, in one sense, "good divorces," in that they are better than the alternative, they aren't "good" in an absolute sense.

"Oftentimes, if you ask the parents they will say the kids are doing just fine, but if you ask the kids they might not agree," Glenn said.

"We found that it is indeed better for parents to have a 'good divorce' than a bad one," he said, "but that having a 'good divorce' seems to only slightly reduce some negative effects of a parental divorce and to reduce others not at all."

In terms of the overall assessment of their pre-adult quality of life, the persons whose parents had a "good divorce" fared more poorly than persons whose parents had a low-conflict, but not happy intact marriage and considerably more poorly than those whose parents had a happy intact marriage.

Grown children of divorce were seven times more likely to agree with the statement, "I was alone a lot as a child." The frequent absence of their parents—whether they were living in another household, working or dating—made a lasting impact.

"One thing that children of divorce have to deal with, particularly if the divorce occurs early in their lives, is the entry and exit of adults other than their biological parents into their lives, such as boyfriends and girlfriends and live-in boyfriends and girlfriends," Glenn said. "They develop emotional attachments with people who sometimes disappear from their lives, which gives the children the feeling that no attachment is secure."

Many respondents noted having to grow up too soon and the feeling of having to carefully negotiate between two parents' worlds—which may have held different beliefs, values and lifestyles. As a result, many children of divorce said they felt divided.

"Many respondents reported that they felt like essentially they had to be different people with their father and their mother," said Glenn. "They had to develop a chameleon personality."

The survey revealed that of those respondents whose parents had a "good divorce," half agreed with the statement, "I always felt like an adult, even when I was a little kid," while more than two-thirds from a bad divorce said the same thing.

Just one-third of young adults from divorced families said that when they were young and needed comfort, they went to one or both of their parents, compared with two-thirds of those with married parents. The grown children of divorce were more likely to have gone to siblings or friends or to have dealt with problems on their own. They also stated a greater need to protect their parents.

In many circumstances, the children kept secrets from one parent about the other, even if they weren't asked to, to circumvent conflict. In other instances, children from divorces were more than twice as likely to be explicitly asked by a parent to keep a secret from the other parent.

The materials from the interviews indicated that even when parents have the very best kind of divorce—in terms of having a friendly and cooperative relationship—negotiating the differences between the mother's world and the father's world leads to confusion and stress among the children and can have lasting consequences.

VIEWPOINT 3

> *"With enough support . . . children are resilient and can come through a divorce stronger and more adept than before."*

Children Can Adapt to Divorce

Donna Olmstead

Donna Olmstead argues in the following viewpoint that children can adapt to divorce if parents minimize their hostility. Joint custody, with fathers playing a stronger role, aids in adjusting to divorce, she says. Collaborative divorce, in which children have a psychotherapist who advocates for their best interest, gives children a voice in the divorce. Citing experts, the author contends that children recover from divorce if the divorcing parents heal their own conflicts. Olmstead writes for the Albuquerque Journal.

As you read, consider the following questions:

1. According to a therapist quoted by the author, how could divorcing parents become happier and more emotionally available to their children than if the parents had stayed married?

Donna Olmstead, "My Two Homes: How Can Children Take Divorce in Stride?" *Albuquerque Journal*, May 6, 2007. Republished with permission of *Albuquerque Journal*, conveyed through Copyright Clearance Center, Inc.-

2. Why, according to experts quoted by the author, do children under the age of five adjust better to divorce?
3. What skills does adapting to divorce teach children, according to the author?

When couples with children divorce, the kids lose the family they have known.

With joint custody the norm, what most children get is two homes—Mom's and Dad's.

They may have two rooms, two sets of clothes, two sets of friends—maybe even two sets of siblings if one or both parents remarry. They may live with two sets of rules.

On the upside, they may celebrate all holidays twice and get double the vacations.

On the downside, children whose parents divorce often experience a decline in economic status. "It's more expensive to maintain two households," says Albuquerque family lawyer Gretchen Walther. "It's just a fact."

If Parents Heal, Children Adjust

And if the parents are still in conflict, the children suffer. Experts say children may be able to adapt after the loss, but not successfully if parents continue to fight, if parents put them in the middle or if one parent disappears from the child's life entirely.

As the leader of the children's support group Banana Splits, Judy Reynolds, a counselor at Enchanted Hills Elementary School in Rio Rancho, helps children with the ups and downs of living two lives.

"Divorce may not ever really be over for these kids," Reynolds says, "but they can return to the safety and peacefulness of their former lives."

Reynolds says the children learn what they can and can't control. "They can't control living in two different households, but maybe they can control where they keep their bike."

To a person, every expert interviewed for this story echoed that how successfully parents heal their rift determines how well their children recover.

"For some of them," Reynolds said, "the calmness that returns to their parents is a real plus. They learn new coping skills."

Joint Custody Helps

Many of the experts—family court judges, family lawyers and family therapists—say several factors make it easier nowadays for children who grow up in divorced families. With joint custody, fathers are playing a stronger role in divorced families, and with collaborative divorce, many couples are able to come through the process without letting the strife between them affect their children, the experts say. Increasingly, courts are recognizing the financial trauma a divorce brings on.

"Things have improved, but we have no magic wand," says Judge Nan Nash, who presides over Second Judicial District Family Court, which handles more than 7,000 cases a year. "Divorce is still traumatic for children."

Divorcing Well

With a 50 percent divorce rate for first-time marriages and 75 percent rate for subsequent marriages, every 30 seconds some child somewhere has parents divorcing, according to *The Collaborative Way to Divorce*, by Stuart G. Webb and Ronald D. Ousky.

According to a progress report posted on the City of Albuquerque Web site, cabq.gov, Bernalillo County had 7.3 divorces for every 1,000 residents in 2001 and 8.2 divorces for every 1,000 residents in 2003.

"How do we do divorce well? It's happening to at least 50 percent of all families," says Margie Polito, a licensed therapist in Albuquerque who specializes in working with children. Polito is focusing her doctoral thesis in counseling psychology

Divorcing Parents Can Help Children Adapt

Constance Ahrons, who studied children of divorce over a 20-year period, found that most children are able to adapt to their parents' divorces. Many even thrive. Her research study illuminates how to foster resilience in children of divorce.

Being told in advance about the planned separation or divorce helps children become more resilient. Parents should decide what they are going to tell their children about the separation or divorce, and they should tell their children together.

Arthur J. Schneider, "Children's Adjustment to Divorce: Fostering Resilience," February 1, 2005. http://missourifamilies.org.

on interviewing families about ways to ensure children of divorce grow up healthy and strong. "If divorce is inevitable, how can we do it in the best way for our children?"

Younger Children Adjust Better

Robert Goodkind, an Albuquerque psychologist who works with families and children, says a goal of therapy for children during divorce is to recognize their parents' split-up as a life experience, but move it out of the realm of a traumatic event. "We don't want the disappointment of the experience to diminish what they do have. Maybe they have two parents who are happier and more emotionally available to them because they aren't caught up in an unhappy marriage."

Judith Lay, an Albuquerque therapist who works with divorcing families, says divorce and subsequent custody arrangements are generally less traumatic on younger children.

Children younger than 5 have less history and attachment invested in their families. "The younger the child, the less loyalty they have to the family as a unit. The older children have a harder adjustment because they are losing their family and they are more loyal to it."

Minimize Parental Hostility

From Polito's experience in more than 30 years of counseling, she sees what doesn't work.

"Kids can go through a divorce and be as OK as kids from intact families, if they aren't exposed to ongoing parental hostility and if the overriding theme is one of cooperation and collaboration," Polito says. "Sadly, many parents let their hostility get in the way of being parents."

Basically, more than time-sharing or child financial support, kids of all ages need their parents to be parents, Polito says. They need to have a secure home with the primary custodial parent and frequent contact and involvement with the noncustodial parent, she says.

"Feeling caught in the middle is corrosive to children," she says.

Nash's advice for divorcing parents? "Get past their conflict and be a parent. I know it's very hard when parents are divorcing not to focus on who's winning and who's losing and being angry at the other person. So parents need to be constantly reminded to focus on the needs of their kids."

Any decision on custody Nash or another judge reaches will never serve the family as well as a decision the parents make, she says. "I say to the parents, 'I don't know your kids and I am never going to know your kids. Nobody can decide their future better than two parents putting their heads together for the best interest of their children.' But I'm going to have to do it, if they can't."

Divorce Causes Financial Hardship

There's no getting around the fact that divorce often causes a financial setback for families. Although researchers disagree about how much a woman's economic status declines after a divorce, most agree women suffer financially and may take as many as five years to recover. A University of Michigan study estimates most women suffer a 30 percent loss of economic status in the first year after a divorce.

Part of the reason is that women don't earn as much as men. In 2005, the median annual earnings of women were 77 percent of those of men, meaning for every dollar a man earns, a woman earns 77 cents, according to the U.S. Census Bureau.

Child support that doesn't address those inequities is to blame, wrote Marsha Garrison in "The Economic Consequences of Divorce," an article for Duke University. Garrison, a law professor at Brooklyn Law School in New York and an advocate for divorce and family law reform, points to the problem: She says it's little or no short-term alimony and child support that fails to ensure a standard of living for the children and their mother equivalent to that of the father.

Collaborative Divorce Best for Children

Walther says the most humane way to end a marriage and preserve the welfare of the children is through a process called collaborative divorce.

Key to collaborative divorce is an agreement not to litigate, but to negotiate with a team of lawyers and psychologists, sometimes a financial adviser. The children have a psychotherapist who advocates for their best interests.

About one-third of her divorces are settled with this approach, rather than litigation, she says. "Litigation in divorce is a lot like surgery in the 1800s. It's pretty archaic."

The support couples receive in a collaborative divorce can start the healing even if the partners are going their separate ways.

"Divorce is maximum stress. It's second on the stress scale to death," she says. "We understand that people can't make good decisions when they are that stressed out, so that's why they have a team to help them."

"What most everyone agrees on is that it's not the divorce per se, but how well the parents get along after the divorce that predicts how messed up the kids are going to be," Walther says. "In a traditional divorce the children don't have a voice. In the collaborative model, they do."

Divorcing Families Return to a Balance

As with all life transitions, divorcing families return to a balance after a period of adjustment, said Reynolds, the school counselor.

Polito observed that children with divorced parents learn to be peacemakers. "They learn to negotiate. They learn to mediate."

Children living in two households also learn organizational skills, Reynolds said. "They have to be good organizers so they don't forget to bring things to school."

The children in Banana Splits learn they aren't the only ones growing up with divorced parents. "Kids are very resilient, and in this group, they learn from one another," Reynolds said. "They learn they still have a mom and dad who love them, even if their mom and dad don't love each other anymore. They learn they didn't do anything to cause the divorce."

With enough support, Polito believes children are resilient and can come through a divorce stronger and more adept than before. "They can be fine adults. They can grow new muscles to adapt. They learn new skills."

> *"Divorce destroys wealth dramatically for both sexes."*

Divorce Causes Poverty

Jay Zagorsky

Jay Zagorsky argues in the following viewpoint that divorce negatively affects accumulation of wealth. Analyzing income, marriage, and divorce data, the author claims that individuals who marry and then divorce end up poorer than those who stay married. The positive effect marriage has on wealth accumulation, he says, applies almost equally to both genders. The negative effect divorce has, he says, affects both genders but affects women more so. Zagorsky is a research scientist at Ohio State University.

As you read, consider the following questions:

1. According to the author's calculations, the average net worth of someone who married and remained married increases from what amount in the first year of marriage to what amount in tenth year of marriage?
2. According to the author, what is the median wealth of a person one decade after being divorced?

Jay Zagorsky, *Journal of Sociology*, vol. 41, December 2005.

3. How do wealth levels of persons who divorced compare to those who remained single, according to the author's analysis?

What impact do marriage and divorce have on wealth? Is divorce as crushing to finances as it is to emotions? Are the finances of married couples more than just the sum of their monetary parts? What are the financial implications of marrying and divorcing multiple times? Investigating these questions is important because so little is known about the causes and consequences of major life events on individuals' and families' financial status. . . .

This article examines the financial impact of these marital changes for . . . the United States. The United States was chosen because it has excellent longitudinal data that track both finances and marital changes. Longitudinal data come from studies that repeatedly survey the same pool of respondents over time. This repeated surveying ensures that results are not skewed by changes in the composition of respondents. It also ensures that key details like short-duration marriages and specific financial value are recorded before respondents forget. . . .

Two Households Versus One Household

Theoretically, becoming married or divorced should have an impact on wealth holdings. One key reason both marriage and divorce affect wealth is because the consumption needs of two adults living together are less than the consumption needs of two separate single adult households. [Linda] Waite after reviewing the cost and benefits of marriage and divorce states: "How does marriage increase wealth? First, economies of scale mean that two can live as cheaply as one—or maybe one and a half" and "[s]econd, because of specialization of spouses in marriage, married people produce more than would the same individuals if single."

Divorce or separation has the opposite effect on wealth. First, since in most US divorce cases the couple's wealth is divided evenly, the act of divorce should halve the amount of wealth over which the individual has control. Additionally, after the divorce occurs a single household of two individuals becomes two separate households. Since the two individuals are now living separately and no longer sharing fixed expenses, their consumption needs rise, causing savings to fall. Hence, divorce should first lower total wealth and then depress future increases since individuals save at a lower rate.

The Expense of Children

While consumption and specialization ideas are persuasive they neglect some important issues, which dampen or reverse the effect of marriage and divorce on wealth. First, the wealth effect of marriage is lower because many people who marry have children, which increases the household's consumption without increasing the household's income, leading to a decrease in savings. As [Joseph] and [Mary] Naifeh show, children are expensive. Even at the poverty line, having another child in a US household costs roughly $300 more per year than having another adult.

Divorce also causes many individuals to reduce their income earning efforts. Many divorce settlements are structured so that the ex-spouse receives a share of the other partner's income. These settlements act as a tax whose revenues are being spent on a good/service that is viewed extremely negatively. Hence, income in these cases falls and savings fall also. Additionally, many divorce cases take an extremely long amount of time and money to settle. This additional expense drives up yearly consumption and drives down savings.

Divorce Causes Entry into the Workforce

Last, both marriage and divorce cause lifestyle changes. These changes can lead individuals to make major changes in their labor force status. For example, in the past many working women who married stopped working to take care of home and family. Currently, many individuals who are not working re-enter the labor force after becoming divorced. These lifestyle changes, by directly affecting income and consumption decisions, alter savings and wealth.

Hence, without looking at data, there is no unambiguous theoretical impact of divorce. . . .

Analysis of the Data

While [a yearly comparison] provides a simple method of showing that wealth differs by marital status, a clearer way to investigate the precise effects is to change from a yearly perspective into an event-based perspective. Instead of focusing on data from 1985 or 1998 this research focuses on two years before being married or one year after becoming divorced. In addition to using an event-based format, the analysis is repeated separately for men and women to see if there are different impacts by gender.

The key data for creating these event histories are the dates when marital status changes. In every survey respondents are allowed to specify up to three different marital changes and are asked to provide the month and year when these changes occurred. These changes are then consolidated into a set of variables created by the survey staff that track the date of all marital changes. After examining all marital status variables, respondents were classified into four groups: single, married once, married then divorced once, and married multiple times. . . . To conserve space this research excludes those married and divorced multiple times. Unfortunately, since the created variables do not track cohabitation or separation these status categories were not formed.

Those Who Stay Married Own More

[Consider] the median net worth of all young baby boomers who never married. Since no marital event change occurred, the base year (year zero) is when the wealth data began in

Divorce Makes Women Poorer

Divorce is a direct cause of poverty for a large proportion of women and their children, although a sizeable proportion of divorces are themselves caused by economic hardship. Once separation takes place, the mother and child unit *becomes* even poorer in these cases. Studies . . . indicate that, in the first year after divorce, and adjusting for family size, women's household income plummets by about 20 to 40 percent while men's declines far less. Even three years after divorce, women's income remains far below what they had during marriage and far below their ex-husbands' current income.

Ann-Marie Ambert,
"Divorce: Facts, Causes and Consequences,"
Contemporary Family Trends,
The Vanier Institute of the Family, 2005.

1985. [There is] a slow and steady increase over time in median wealth. The combined median increases from around $1500 in year zero (1985) to $10,900 by the fifteenth year (2000), an increase of almost seven times. Overall males who never married had slightly more wealth than females who never married since the male median is on average 1.6 times larger and the male amount is larger in all but one year.

[Consider] how median net worth changes for young baby boomers who married and remained married as of the latest survey. From eleven years before marriage until one year before marriage the growth in net worth is almost identical to the path followed by individuals who were always single. Eleven years before marriage net worth was only $3900 and it grew to slightly more than $10,000 the year before marriage. In the year of marriage wealth fell to less than $8000 and then started climbing rapidly. In year two net worth was over $15,000 and increased to a peak of almost $43,000 by the tenth year of marriage.

Among married couples there were no dramatic wealth differences based on the respondent's sex. Like individuals who were always single, prior to marriage males had slightly more wealth than females, with the male median about 1.7 times larger than the female. After marriage the situation reverses and male respondents' net worth was approximately 90 percent of female respondents. One reason for this is that females in the [survey] sample tended to have older spouses, while married males in the [survey] sample tended to have younger spouses. In the entire sample, the average female respondent married a man born in 1958, while the average male married a female born in 1962. Since wealth holdings are directly related to age, married females have higher wealth than married males because their partners have, on average, four more years to save.

Married Once, Then Divorced

[Consider] how median net worth changes for young baby boomers who married once and then divorced. Individuals are included in this picture only from the time they first married, not while they were single. Even many years prior to divorce, couples whose marriage breaks up do not build up wealth like families that stay united. Looking back over the entire marital history shows that per person wealth is less than $10,000.

[Analysis of the data] shows that wealth started falling four years (median $8918) before the divorce and bottomed out the year prior to the divorce (median $3452). This steady reduction is due to many couples separating prior to divorce. [Researchers Matthew] Bramlett and [William] Mosher track the time from first separation to divorce for a random sample of all US couples and show that in 1995 one-third of all couples who separated divorced within six months, 54 percent of all couples who separated divorced within a year, 75 percent of all couples who separated divorced within two years and 88 percent of all couples divorced within four years. While not all divorces are preceded by separations and not all separations lead to divorce, data in [researchers Rose] Kreider and [Jason] Fields suggest a high correlation between the two acts. Since divorce is often the culmination of a long process, wealth falls for many couples long before the marriage is legally voided.

Slight Recovery After Divorce

Wealth begins climbing in the year of the divorce (up to $4175). Nevertheless, the climb is not large since even a decade after divorce, the median wealth stays below $10,000. The overall picture of those who divorce is one of a low initial wealth build-up, a steady decline starting well before divorce occurs, a bottoming out prior to the divorce and then a small but modest recovery following divorce.

Comparing the effects of divorce on males and females visually shows that men do financially better. Prior to divorce the average male wealth was lower than female wealth (average 0.7 times). After divorce the typical male held 2.5 times the amount of wealth held by the typical female. While this seems large in percentage terms, the difference in absolute dollars after divorce ($5124) is relatively small. While men come out slightly ahead, divorce destroys wealth dramatically for both sexes. . . .

Marriage Creates Wealth

How do marriage and divorce affect wealth? This research provided a number of theories that show marital status changes could have an impact on wealth both positively and negatively. Using longitudinal data, the experiences of US young baby boomers were examined. Regression results show that for respondents who married and stay married, per person net worth was 93 percent higher than for single respondents. Moreover, these married respondents' wealth increased on average by 16 percent per year, the highest of any marital status group.

[Survey] respondents who divorced had the exact opposite experience. Divorce is associated with wealth levels that were 77 percent lower than those experienced by single respondents and divorced individuals experienced annual increases of just 14 percent per year. Single respondents' wealth levels lie between the married and divorced, but showed annual increases (8 percent) that were the smallest of all groups.

This research also investigated the impact of marriage and divorce by gender. Regression results, which are in percentage terms, show that men made out financially better than women in both marriage and divorce. Nevertheless, the graphs show that when the results are measured in absolute dollars, the difference between the sexes is qualitatively insignificant.

Many other developed countries are experiencing the same trends in marriage and divorce rates as the United States. Do the results identified by this research hold up for these other countries? While a definitive answer is not yet known, future research using non-US longitudinal data should also find a positive marriage and a negative divorce impact on individuals' finances.

Viewpoint 5

"Being divorced has long-term negative consequences for physical health that are not immediately visible but become visible later in life."

Divorce Harms Women's Health

Fredrick O. Lorenz, K.A.S. Wickrama, Rand D. Conger, and Glen H. Elder Jr.

Fredrick O. Lorenz, K.A.S. Wickrama, Rand D. Conger, and Glen H. Elder Jr. argue in the following viewpoint that divorce and conditions resulting from divorce create chronic stress in women which, in turn, harms their physical health. The authors contend that while the psychological distress may decline, a physical effect can appear years after the divorce. Divorce, they say, is a chronic stressor. In addition, the authors claim, divorce leaves mothers vulnerable to an accumulation of stressful life events that undermine physical health. Lorenz and Wickrama are professors at Iowa State University. Conger is a professor at University of California, and Elder is a professor at University of North Carolina.

As you read, consider the following questions:

1. Over longer periods of time, how does the experience of being divorced affect women, especially mothers, in the view of the authors?
2. According to the authors, how does chronic stress affect the number of acute physical ailments one experiences?
3. According to the authors, how do single mothers and married mothers differ in the number of health problems they report?

We hypothesize that divorce immediately increases psychological distress and has long-term negative consequences for the physical health of divorced people. In addition, we hypothesize that divorce indirectly causes long-term increases in distress through stressful midlife events. The hypotheses are tested using data from 416 rural Iowa women who were interviewed repeatedly in the early 1990s when they were mothers of adolescent children; the women were interviewed again in 2001. The data support the hypotheses. In the years immediately after their divorce (1991–1994), divorced women reported significantly higher levels of psychological distress than married women but no differences in physical illness. A decade later (in 2001), the divorced women reported significantly higher levels of illness, even after controlling for age, remarriage, education, income, and prior health. Compared to their married counterparts, divorced women reported higher levels of stressful life events between 1994 and 2000, which led to higher levels of depressive symptoms in 2001.

Is Divorce a Chronic Stressor?

Divorce is one of the most pervasive personal disruptions in Western culture. Although divorce rates in the United States have been dropping since the 1970s "decade of divorce," they remain higher than in most European countries and dramatically higher than the rates reported in earlier eras. Divorce among parents is a special policy concern because single motherhood (or absent fatherhood) is often cited as an important cause of crime, delinquency, and community decline. At the individual level, divorce is associated with economic hardship, social isolation, and risky health behaviors among both adults and children. Divorce has long been linked to physical and emotional health problems.

Scholars have made remarkable progress in synthesizing knowledge about the dynamics of marriage and the consequences of divorce. In the process, they have isolated continuing points of inquiry common to both health and family sociologists, two of which are addressed in this study. One is whether divorce is better understood as an acute stressor or as a chronic stressor. Some studies suggest that divorce is a temporary crisis to which most people adapt within two or three years, while others see it as a persistent chronic state.

The second point of inquiry focuses on differences in the timing and duration of psychological distress and physical health problems in the years after divorce. Studies have shown that divorce has large effects on psychological distress but smaller effects on physical health perhaps because physical illnesses accumulate slowly over time in response to divorce's chronic dimension. Direct comparisons of the changes in distress and illness are seldom made, however, because modeling change requires longitudinal data and because most previous studies have not included both outcomes in a single model.

This study traces the decade-long (1991–2001) effects of divorce on the psychological distress and physical illness of a panel of 416 women who were mothers of ninth graders in 1991. In the process, we delineate several hypotheses. The first is that *getting a divorce* is disruptive and elevates the psychological distress of family members. Over longer periods of time, however, *the experience of being divorced* leaves many individuals, especially mothers, in chronically disadvantaged social and economic circumstances, and these chronic circum-

Stress Can Make Women Sick

While stress is not considered an illness, it can cause specific medical symptoms, often serious enough to send women to the emergency room or their health care professional's office. In fact, 43 percent of adults suffer adverse health effects from stress, and 75 to 90 percent of all physician office visits have stress-related components, according to the American Psychological Association.

National Women's Health Resource Center, "Stress," May 25, 2005. www.healthywomen.org.

stances have cumulative adverse effects on physical health. The third hypothesis argues that divorce also has longer-term effects on psychological distress, but these effects are primarily indirect through the stressful life events to which the divorced are especially susceptible.

Psychological Effect Is Acute

A number of perspectives have been proposed to understand the consequences of divorce for individuals, including life course and crisis theories. One approach that resonates with many health and family sociologists is the divorce-stress-adjustment perspective, which views divorce as a process that begins with feelings of estrangement from one's spouse, continues as one or both spouses decide to separate, and then is followed by adjustment after divorce. This perspective shares much with the broader "stress-distress" paradigm in health sociology by conceiving of divorce as a stressor to which individuals adapt with varying degrees of resilience, depending in part on the social and economic resources at their disposal. . . .

One distinctive contribution of the divorce-stress-adjustment perspective is that it identifies two competing models of adjustment after divorce. The *crisis model* views divorce as a disturbance from which most people recover, whereas the *chronic stress model* sees divorce as a major role change that ushers in new levels of chronic stress, especially among single mothers. These two models of adjustment have parallels in the distinction between acute and chronic stress as articulated by the stress-distress paradigm, and they suggest a fundamental distinction between the relatively short-term and long-term effects of divorce on psychological distress and physical illness. Specifically, Wheaton defined acute events—such as getting divorced—as stressors with identifiable beginnings and endings. In its idealized form, the intensity of an acute event is presumed to peak quickly and then recede precipitously. Psychological distress is expected to follow a similarly ephemeral pattern in response, rising quickly and then atrophying over time. Our first hypothesis builds on the crisis model of adjustment:

> *Hypothesis 1*: Trajectories of psychological distress correspond closely to the event of getting a divorce, rising quickly as the divorce unfolds and then declining as it recedes into the past. . . .

Physical Health Effects Become Visible Later

Chronic stressors, such as those associated with being a single mother, are less "time-limiting" than acute events, and decades of research has demonstrated that chronic stress can have cumulative effects on physical health through an interconnected set of cardiovascular, neurological, and immunological mechanisms most recently summarized by [William] Lovallo. Chronic stressors may increase the number of acute physical ailments one experiences, and these may come and go, but chronic stress may also accelerate the onset of chronic physical health conditions such as heart and respiratory ailments, diabetes, and hypertension. Many of these conditions take years to develop and then do not disappear when the source of chronic stress disappears.

For many women, divorce signals the onset of chronic disadvantage caused by the social isolation and economic hardship incumbent upon the role of single mother. Family incomes of divorced women are estimated to be 13 to 35 percent lower than for married women, even when there were no income differences between women in the two groups before the separation. Single mothers also report more health problems than do married mothers. Thus, our second hypothesis . . . is as follows:

> *Hypothesis 2*: Being divorced has long-term negative consequences for physical health that are not immediately visible but become visible later in life.

In contrast, we do not expect divorce to have a direct effect on psychological distress a decade later.

Stress in Divorced Women Accumulates over Time

One difficulty facing researchers is distinguishing changes in psychological distress and physical illness that are due to divorce from changes that are due to the accumulation of more proximal events for which divorce can be a catalyst. Recently divorced mothers must often take on new jobs or increase their hours on existing jobs. In rural areas, these may be marginal or low-paying jobs in industries that provide few benefits. Divorce frequently entails moving to an inferior residence, which may leave one vulnerable to costly home repairs. The children of recently divorced mothers are more likely to change schools, and changing schools may lead to academic and social adjustment problems, dropping out of school before graduating, associating with deviant peers, and delinquent behaviors. Thus, we expect the average number (level) of stressful life events to be higher among divorced women than among married women five to ten years after divorce, with the rate of accumulation of these events possibly even accelerating over time. This hypothesized proliferation of stressful events in the years following divorce . . . form[s] the third hypothesis:

> *Hypothesis 3*: Change in status from married to divorced leaves many mothers susceptible to an accumulation of stressful life events that elevate distress and undermine physical health. . . .

Divorce Produces Chronic Stress

The results . . . are consistent with our hypotheses and offer insights into how the crisis and chronic stress models of adjustment to divorce . . . might complement rather than compete with one another. . . .

The observed increases followed by declines in depressive symptoms in the years immediately after divorce suggest that psychological distress is indeed more volatile than physical illness, and the crisis model may best apply to more volatile outcomes. In contrast, if *being divorced* is a chronic stressor because of the longer-term economic hardship and social isolation it causes, then the observed changes in illness over the decade can be understood to be a cumulative response to chronic conditions.

> *"It's nearly impossible to go through a divorce and have it not impact your work life."*

Employees' Divorce Harms Employers

Margarita Bauza

Margarita Bauza argues in the following viewpoint that an employee's divorce harms his or her employer. She maintains that stress from the divorce and necessary time off work cost the employer dollars. In addition, she says, the distractions cause by the financial and emotional issues associated with divorce affect work performance. Employees also may spread their anger and bitterness about the divorce throughout the workplace. She says that employee assistance programs and empathy can help. Bauza writes for the Detroit Free Press.

As you read, consider the following questions:

1. According to a study cited by the author, how much does stress from relationship-related issues cost employers annually?

Margarita Bauza, "Emotional Toll of Employee Divorce May Cost Companies Dearly," *Detroit Free Press*, February 13, 2007. Reprinted by permission of the *Detroit Free Press*.

2. According to a study cited by the author, how many hours of employee work time were lost annually in the year following the employee's divorce?
3. According to a lawyer quoted by the author, what special privileges are employers required to give divorcing employees?

When John Casey's wife filed for divorce a year and a half ago, he immediately worried about how he'd stay on top of his high-stakes career.

Casey, then the managing director of a public relations company, added a heavy dose of litigation, custody battles and financial maneuvering to an already hectic schedule.

"I had days at work where I'd be on a natural high after hitting a home run and came back to an e-mail at the office from an attorney that sucked the wind right out of me," said Casey, 42, of Waterford, Mich., who at the time supervised 25 employees at the Detroit offices of Strat@comm.

Divorce Impacts Work

As candy, roses and other romantic gifts pour into the nation's offices Wednesday [for Valentine's Day, February 14, 2007], there is a quiet epidemic simmering in the hearts of millions of workers across the country. With more than 50 percent of marriages ending in divorce nationally, studies show that breakups increasingly harm the workplace.

"It's nearly impossible to go through a divorce and have it not impact your work life," said Karen McDonald, Casey's divorce attorney and a partner at the law firm of Jaffe Raitt Heuer & Weiss PC in Southfield, Mich. "Aside from the immediate toll it takes, you're going to be involved in a litigation that requires you take time off of work."

Employees getting divorced must balance legal, financial, housing and child care decisions. They typically spend a large amount of time and energy finding a lawyer, revising household budgets, looking for a new place to live and making child care arrangements.

Divorce Distracts Employees

"The process of getting divorced is an emotional roller coaster, and that impacts people's ability to be mindful on the job," says Bev Smallwood, a workplace psychologist from Hattiesburg, Miss. "When people are distracted, they make more mistakes and work more slowly. If they're feeling depressed, their creativity will be down. If they're feeling angry, they may project some of that anger onto co-workers or even customers."

Meanwhile, practical demands can cut into work time. Employees getting divorced face a seemingly endless stream of legal, financial, housing and child care decisions. Vast amounts of time and energy are often consumed by finding a lawyer, revising the household budget, looking for an apartment, making new child care arrangements—and the list goes on.

Linda Wasmer Andrews,
"Coping with Divorce: Help Maintain Your Employees' Workplace Productivity During a Personal Crisis,"
HR Magazine, *May 1, 2005.*

What that means for the other workers is a potential loss of productivity, dealing with a moodier boss or co-worker and, in some cases, picking up the slack for someone who is distracted or must be out of the office to deal with divorce matters.

Calculating the Cost

A 2006 study by Minneapolis-based Life Innovations titled "Marriage & Family Wellness: Corporate America's Business?" calculated that:

- Stress from relationship-related issues cost companies $300 billion a year.
- In the year after a divorce, employees lost an average of more than 168 hours of work time, according to a 2005 study by Richard Mueller, a researcher at the University of Lethbridge in Alberta, Canada.
- Unhappily married couples are almost four times more likely to have a partner abusing alcohol than happily married couples, according to a 2006 study in *Journal of Family Psychology*.
- Financial pressures typically worsen for employees going through divorce, the cost of which can range from $15,000 to $30,000.

Because of this, many employees have to adjust to a major change in their standard of living. "These challenges are not the kind to be resolved overnight," said Joshua Estrin, a licensed psychotherapist based in Ft. Lauderdale, Fla. "The divorce process can take anywhere from a few months to several years."

Effects Not Always Obvious

Unlike other life-altering events—such as illness or the death of a loved one—the effects of divorce are not always obvious, said Matthew Turvey, a Minneapolis-based researcher with the marriage-focused not-for-profit Life Innovations.

Yet the impact is just as emotionally wrenching and time consuming.

"Companies focus so much on productivity that we forget that a happy employee is a productive employee," Turvey said.

Robert Pasick, a clinical psychologist and professor at the University of Michigan's William Davidson Institute, said it's common for employees going through divorce to appear angry and bitter, and to spread those feelings at work.

"I think employee assistance programs, counseling, church groups and things like that are all helpful," Pasick said. "You shouldn't draw people at work into conversations about this. It's not a place to get sympathy or to badmouth your significant other—it's disruptive."

Casey, the executive who divorced last year, said communicating closely with his attorney and his employer helped him minimize the strain at work.

Empathy Helps

Going through a breakup has made him a more compassionate manager, he said. He now owns Casey Communications, a public relations firm. A current employee of his recently divorced and faces lingering issues.

"It never stops," he said. "I know. I think when you go through this yourself you see the havoc firsthand. It helps you care for your employees and empathize more."

Nevertheless, employers are not required to give divorcing employees special privileges, said Thomas Williams, an attorney who works with McDonald, Casey's attorney.

Workers must remember that they still need to get the job done despite the breakup, Williams said.

"All employers want employees to come to work on time and be at work and do a great job each day," he said. "Though our clients are sympathetic, they are also most interested that work is done properly and on time."

Periodical Bibliography

The following articles have been selected to supplement the diverse views presented in this chapter.

Constance R. Ahrons	"Family Ties After Divorce: Long-Term Implications for Children," *Family Process*, March 1, 2007.
Espen Bratberg and Sigve Tjotte	"Income Effects of Divorce in Families with Dependent Children," *Journal of Population Economics*, vol. 21, no. 2, April 2008.
Jennifer L. Bratter and Rosalind B. King	"But Will It Last?: Marital Instability Among Interracial and Same-Race Couples," *Family Relations*, April, 2008.
David Crary	"Divorce Rate Lowest Since 1970," *Sunday Gazette-Mail*, June 3, 2007.
Pauline Jelinek	"Military Divorce Rate Holding Steady," *AP Online*, March 1, 2008.
Gregory Karp	"Divorce Breaks Pocketbooks, as Well as Hearts," *Morning Call*, July 9, 2006.
Jennifer Hickes Lundquist	"A Comparison of Civilian and Enlisted Divorce Rates During the Early All Volunteer Force Era," *Journal of Political and Military Sociology*, December 1, 2007.
Albertine J. Oldehikel, Johan Ormel, Rene Veenstra, Andrea F. Winter, and Frank C. Verhulst	"Parental Divorce and Offspring Depressive Symptoms: Dutch Developmental Trends During Early Adolescence," *Journal of Marriage & Family*, vol. 70, no. 2, May 2008.
Hugh O'Neill	"The New Occupational Hazard: Divorce," *Prevention*, vol. 56, no. 7, July 2004.
Jay Teachman	"Complex Life Course Patterns and the Risk of Divorce in Second Marriages," *Journal of Marriage & Family*, vol. 70, no. 2, May 2008.
Anna M. Tinsley	"Marriages Dissolving at Lowest Rate Since 1970," *Fort Worth Star-Telegram*, May 11, 2007.

CHAPTER 2

Can Divorce Be Prevented?

Chapter Preface

What role does poverty play in causing divorce? The effect of poverty may be both direct and indirect.

A 2008 Roper Poll found that among currently married Americans who have considered divorce, the primary reasons for thinking about it were issues surrounding children (19 percent) and fears about cheating (18 percent). Among those who actually had divorced, however, the number one reason given for divorce (36 percent of those surveyed) was verbal or physical abuse.

What does this have to do with poverty? The U.S. Department of Justice (DOJ) has noted a significant link between poverty and increased incidences of domestic violence. The DOJ reported that in 1992–1993 women with an annual family income of under $10,000 were more likely to report having experienced violence by an intimate partner than those with incomes over $10,000. A 2002 study published by the National Center for Children in Poverty found that "there is a growing body of evidence indicating a higher prevalence of domestic violence among the welfare population. This suggests that poverty may increase women's vulnerability to abuse."

The second most common reason given for divorce in the 2008 Roper poll was money (22 percent). A 2004 study in Australia also found that financial hardship was a major cause for family breakdown. An earlier Australian study found that among men who had ever been married, men with incomes below $15,600 were more than twice as likely to have divorced than were men with incomes between $52,000 and $78,000.

While divorce rates have generally fallen, sociology professor Beau Weston observed in 2007 that "the divorce rate has not fallen among the least educated. The growing marriage divide is becoming a class divide" and "poor people are more likely to divorce." . . .

Poverty itself makes marriage less stable. Researcher David J. Fein of Abt Associates, Inc., has observed that economically disadvantaged persons are as likely to marry as other people "but their marriages are substantially more unstable." Fein says that "the difficulty of staying married increases substantially with levels of economic disadvantage." He says the likelihood of splitting up is consistently higher for women with less education or who live in less affluent neighborhoods. "The effect of neighborhood income level is especially large," he says. "For example, the probability of breaking up within ten years of marriage is nearly twice as high for women from the bottom quarter (44 percent breakup) as for those from the top quarter (23 percent breakup) of neighborhoods ranked by median family income."

Can couples overcome the disadvantages that seem to be attached to poverty? Some believe that teaching people how to have successful marriages can prevent divorce. Poverty, however, may hinder the ability to successfully utilize such instruction. Gordon Berlin, executive vice president of social policy research organization MDRC, stated in 2004 congressional testimony that evidence suggests that "marital education, family counseling, and related services can improve middle-class couples' communication and problem-solving skills, resulting initially in greater marital satisfaction and, in some cases, reduced divorce, although these effects appear to fade over time." It was not clear, in his opinion, whether such education would reduce marital stress and eventual divorce among low-income populations, due to other stressors that middle-class families do not face.

While it is often said that money cannot buy happiness, poverty appears to stress marriage in ways that increase the likelihood of divorce.

VIEWPOINT 1

"If spouses enter marriage with the belief that divorce is the solution to any problems that arise, 'their marriages are of significantly lower quality and thus often end in divorce.'"

Covenant Marriage Can Prevent Divorce

Katherine Shaw Spaht

Katherine Shaw Spaht argues in the following viewpoint that covenant marriage creates greater commitment to marriage and makes divorce less likely. Lawyers, she contends, favor no-fault divorce because it makes family law practice lucrative. The argument that no-fault divorce would reduce acrimony, Spaht says, has proven unfounded. She maintains that covenant marriage has been proven to increase commitment to and satisfaction with marriage. Spaht is a professor at Louisiana State University Law Center.

As you read, consider the following questions:

1. What three principal characteristics do covenant marriage statutes in Louisiana, Arizona, and Arkansas contain, according to the author?

Katherine Shaw Spaht, "Covenant Marriage: An Achievable Legal Response to the Inherent Nature of Marriage and its Various Goods," *Ave Maria Law Review*, June 22, 2006. Reproduced by permission.

2. What example does the author give for the argument that no-fault divorce has not eliminated acrimony in divorce proceedings involving children?
3. According to the author, which spouse has the right and duty to manage the household in covenant marriage?

Marriage in the United States during the last fifty years has been understood as a private contract, "grounded in new cultural and constitutional norms of sexual liberty and privacy." Marriage formation rules were simplified with virtually no requirements for waiting periods, publication of banns, or requisite public celebration. Dissolution rules were simplified by the introduction of unilateral no-fault divorce accompanied by streamlined procedures for divorce that significantly hastened dissolution of marriages. A divorce can now be obtained upon the simple petition of either party, which is touted as means to the end of a "clean break" from the other spouse. And, as at least one observer commented: "America's experiment with the private contractual model of marriage has failed on many counts and accounts—with children and women bearing the primary costs."

A Preferable Form of Marriage

As a legal response to the social costs levied by the streamlined divorce system, three states have adopted covenant-marriage statutes that offer couples an optional—and I argue preferable—form of marriage. Covenant marriage imposes obligations upon husband and wife to prepare for marriage and to take "reasonable steps" to preserve their marriage if difficulties arise. Divorce, in the covenant marriage context, generally requires proof of serious fault on the part of one spouse or a lengthy waiting period of living separate and apart. The statutes adopted by Louisiana, Arizona, and Arkansas share three principal characteristics: (1) mandatory premarital counseling by a religious cleric or professional marriage counselor about the seriousness of marriage; (2) the execution of a Declaration of Intent (the covenant or agreement containing their promises)—a legal obligation to take reasonable steps to preserve the marriage if marital difficulties arise (in at least one state, this obligation explicitly lasts until divorce); and (3) limited grounds for divorce, consisting of serious fault on the part of one spouse or, in the absence of such fault, a significant period of time living separate and apart. In Louisiana, the legislation governing a covenant marriage also includes special obligations imposed upon a covenant couple during their covenant marriage that are not imposed upon other married couples. These obligations include: (1) to love and respect each other; (2) to live together; (3) to make decisions relating to family life in the best interest of the family; (4) to maintain and teach their children "in accordance with their capacities, natural inclinations, and aspirations"; and (5) the right and duty of each spouse to manage the household. . . .

Lawyers Support No-Fault Divorce

In their insistence that marriage is simply one of many varieties of intimate adult relationships without moral content (which inherently requires making a moral judgment), legal elites find family law bar members to be their strongest allies. Content with divorce law practice stripped of fault and the trial of such allegations, the family law bar resists any return to marriage law with moral content. Much of this resistance stems from the fact that, since 1970, no-fault divorce law has been a financial boon to an increasing number of lawyers.

No-fault divorce means that a lawyer need not allege a fault ground for divorce and prove it by factual evidence designed to fit within jurisprudential interpretations of what constitutes adultery, cruel treatment, or habitual intemperance. There is no need to extensively interview the spouse, friends, and family, to hire investigators, or to marshal credible testimony—actions designed to be distasteful and, consequently, deter people from divorcing. Accordingly, no such evidence will be offered by the defendant in response to allegations in the plaintiff's petition. The petition may simply allege that plaintiff desires a divorce because of irreconcilable differences or irretrievable breakdown of the marriage. Most significantly, no defense exists absent reconciliation, allowing the plaintiff's attorney to accomplish the desired result for his client (unlike the experience of lawyers prior to the enactment of no-fault divorce who often were unsuccessful in obtaining a divorce for fault of the other spouse) without the expenditure of time previously required to gather the factual evidence necessary to establish fault. Not surprisingly, the history of the passage of no-fault divorce legislation indicates that members of the legal profession, in cooperation with legal elites, were the primary moving force behind no-fault divorce reform.

Economically, no-fault divorce meant that a divorce law practice could finally be feasible, if not very lucrative. Until the widespread adoption of no-fault divorce in the United States in the mid-1970s, very few, if any, lawyers specialized in the practice of divorce law. Lawyers simply could not sustain a practice economically by handling only divorce cases. The law required proof of serious fault by the other spouse, and obtaining such demanding factual evidence was both unattractive and expensive. Accordingly, an attorney could not charge his client a sufficient amount to be adequately compensated for the time and resources expended. Meanwhile, a client in the throes of a divorce loses resources once provided by the other spouse (lost economies of scale); therefore, a divorce case client rarely possessed the ability to pay the hourly sum a lawyer justifiably could charge for his time and effort. Due to these financial strains, lawyers were forced to balance their divorce practice with cases in other areas of the law.

Divorces Still Acrimonious and Unsavory

Since the 1970s, family law specialization has increased exponentially. What the lawyer may be forced to try in a divorce case is ordinarily limited to economic matters, such as alimony or division of marital property. The matter of child support has now been reduced to a mechanical calculation of a sum based upon specific guidelines. Nonetheless, contrary to what opponents of reform claim, not all unsavory divorce matters, especially egregious fault committed by a spouse, have been eliminated from judicial consideration. Rather than alleging fault on the part of the other spouse to obtain the divorce, today a more pernicious form of family law litigation has emerged: contested child custody cases containing allegations of sexual or physical abuse. This form of litigation has proliferated such that many veteran family law practitioners express deep concern about its effect on families and society at large. The injustice to one spouse of being repudiated by the other spouse, who is often the one who has breached the marital relationship by a serious fault, occurs without an opportunity to express indignation publicly and to seek redress. Is it preferable for the spouses to direct indignation toward each other as a reason to gain sole custody of a child, rather than direct anger against each other as grounds for divorce?

Any claim by the legal profession that no-fault divorce reduces the acrimony that once existed in divorce proceedings rings hollow. The acrimony that exists between divorcing spouses continues unabated and, unfortunately, most often appears not in the divorce proceeding itself but in the ancillary matter of child custody. The reward for a successful physical or sexual abuse claim—no visitation or severely restricted visitation by the abusing parent—is significant. Proving such allegations, however, usually requires a physical examination of the child. How could divorce proceedings be more distasteful than custody contests in which allegations are made against a parent that necessitate a gynecological or urological examination of a child?

Covenant Marriage Is Option for Commitment

Recognition of the opponents to divorce reform and knowledge of their arguments better equips the individuals who encourage and support divorce law reform. One of the most attractive features of covenant marriage as a divorce reform . . . is its optional nature. No one seeks to impose upon other citizens her "religion" or her understanding of marriage viewed through the prism of natural law. Reform advocates who promote covenant marriage simply propose permitting citizens the ability to choose a more committed form of marriage that is entered into only after serious deliberation. Legal academicians need not choose it for themselves, and family lawyers need not represent covenant spouses seeking a divorce.

Covenant marriage statutes in Louisiana, Arizona, and Arkansas contain three general features: (1) mandatory premarital counseling about the seriousness of marriage and the intention of the couple that it be lifelong; (2) the legal obligation to take all reasonable steps to preserve the couple's marriage if marital difficulties arise; and (3) restricted grounds for divorce consisting of fault on the part of the other spouse or a significant period of time living separate and apart. Thus, covenant marriage tightens the rules on entry into marriage as well as exit from marriage. At the same time, this reform option seeks to strengthen the marriage during its existence by imposing a legal responsibility to try to preserve the marriage upon the spouses, a responsibility that they agreed to in advance.

Premarital Counseling and Promises

Mandatory premarital counseling in a covenant marriage may be performed by a member of the clergy or a professional marriage counselor, which permits Catholic Pre-Cana programs of preparation for engaged couples to constitute satisfaction of this statutory requirement. In cities with a Community Marriage Covenant or Policy ("CMP") signed by clergy in the community, signatories ordinarily agree to: (1) a minimum number of counseling sessions with the minister or priest; (2) a premarital inventory such as PREPARE or FOCCUS (Facilitating Open Couple Communication, Understanding, and Study); and (3) the guarantee of a mentoring couple assigned to the engaged couple. When the premarital counseling ends, the couple signs a document called a Declaration of Intent that contains the content of their covenant. In Louisiana, the Declaration includes the agreement to take reasonable steps to preserve the marriage as well as the couple's agreement to be bound by the Louisiana law of covenant marriage (choice-of-law clause). Both spouses sign the agreement and then execute an affidavit, signed by a notary, attesting to having received the required counseling and having read the Covenant Marriage Act. In their Declaration of Intent, the couple agrees in advance to take steps to preserve the marriage, a legal obligation which begins when marital difficulties arise and "should continue" until rendition of the divorce judgment. Clearly, a covenant couple understands that their commitment to marriage is stronger by virtue of the time necessary to plan and complete this process. Research suggests that the attitudes of spouses upon entry into marriage ultimately determines marriage quality; if spouses enter marriage with the belief that divorce is the solution to any problems that arise, "their marriages are of significantly lower quality and thus often end in divorce."

Duty of Love and Respect

During a Louisiana covenant marriage, spouses owe to each other not only the explicit obligations of fidelity (not to share one's sexual potential with another and to affirmatively submit to the reasonable sexual desires of the other), support (to provide the other with not only the necessities of life but its conveniences), and assistance (to cooperate in the tasks resulting from a life in common, including to help an ill or infirm spouse), but also explicit legal obligations unique to covenant couples. Six special provisions borrowed from other countries add depth to the covenant for Louisiana covenant couples. Not all of the provisions reflect the traditional role of law—to constrain or punish. Instead, some of these provisions simply

Covenant Marriage Makes Bonds More Secure

Supporters of the movement claim that couples are motivated to join in a Covenant Marriage as a way to make their bonds more secure. "There have been primarily two large groups getting involved in Covenant Marriage," [Louisiana Senator Tony] Perkins explains. "You have those who came from broken homes; they understand the pain of divorce, and how fragile the marital relationship is. You also have people who have experienced divorce and don't want to go through it again. The increase in cohabitation shows that a lot of couples have foregone marriage out of fear that there's no protection in it. Covenant Marriage offers this sort of protection: the power shifts from the spouse who wants out to the spouse who wants to maintain the marriage."

Jeffrey Cottrill, "Covenant Marriage," Divorce Magazine.com, *2008. www.divorcemag.com.*

teach and exhort, the so-called expressive function of law. The first provision directs that "spouses [in a covenant marriage] owe each other love and respect and they commit to a community of living. Each spouse should attend to the satisfaction of the other's needs." Essentially, in a covenant marriage, the law interprets the spouses' commitment as one to a "community of living." Marriage, the foundation of the family, is described by the law as a community in which each spouse is obligated to love and respect (deferential regard) the other and attend to the other's needs—such requirements strongly reflect notions of mutual giving and sacrificial love.

Second, a covenant marriage is a marriage of equal regard: each spouse has the right and the duty to manage the household. Third, determining where the covenant couple shall live requires mutual consent, "according to [both] their requirements and those of the family." By treating the couple as a couple ("their requirements") and the family as a unit, covenant marriage appears to reject the radical autonomy of the individual, hence what Cardinal [Lopez] Trujillo describes as the freedom of the individual. Fourth, covenant spouses, after collaboration, "shall make decisions relating to family life in the best interest of the family." Again, the family as a unit takes center stage, implying that more people are involved, not simply the couple themselves. The final requirement directly refers to those other people: "[t]he spouses are bound to maintain, to teach, and to educate their children born of the marriage in accordance with their capacities, natural inclinations, and aspirations, and shall prepare them for their future." Children, the other individually unique people, are welcomed in a covenant marriage, and the law affirms their centrality to a covenant marriage.

Divorce Requires Grounds

Not only does the law directly regulate covenant marriage by describing its content, it also indirectly governs the conduct of covenant couples toward each other and the family by prescribing "fault" grounds for divorce. One spouse can obtain a divorce or legal separation from the other spouse by proving that the other spouse committed adultery, was convicted of a felony, physically or sexually abused the plaintiff spouse or a child of the parties, or abandoned the spouse for a year. Otherwise, to obtain a divorce, the spouses must live separate and apart for two years. Thus, inferentially, the grounds for divorce speak to the appropriate conduct of the spouses during a covenant marriage: each spouse is to "yield to the other in sexual matters as long as the request [is] reasonable and to conduct himself so as not to bring dishonor and shame to the family formed by the marriage, which could occur by adulterous affairs, outrageous or felonious behavior, and constant intemperance."

Women Lead in Selecting Covenant Marriage

With the enactment of the first covenant marriage statute in Louisiana in 1997, Steven L. Nock began an empirical study entitled "Can Louisiana's Covenant Marriage Law Solve America's Divorce Problem?" The five-year study yielded a wealth of information that "offers a glimpse of the effect of cultural changes on the understanding of marriage, as well as the self-selection effects of [the covenant marriage] experiment and the sanctification of marriage created by the choice of a more committed form of marriage." A Gallup poll conducted in 1998 to measure the attitudes of a random sample of citizens in Louisiana began the study. Next, the research team identified six hundred newly married couples, fifty percent covenant and fifty percent standard married couples, and observed them over a five-year period.

In comparing covenant and standard couples, Nock and his research team identified women as the leaders in selecting covenant marriage, "particularly women with a vested interest in childbearing who apparently fe[lt] the need for the protection of stronger divorce laws." Men led in selecting "standard" marriage. Covenant couples were more educated, held more traditional attitudes, and expressed the conviction that their choice of a covenant marriage was very important. The results also indicated that covenant couples [were] "far more likely to choose communication strategies that do not revolve around attacking or belittling their partner. They [were] less likely to respond to conflict with sarcasm or hostility, two communication strategies that [John] Gottman indicate[d] [were] particularly strongly associated with poor marriage outcomes."

Covenant Marriages Proven Better

In follow-up surveys two years after marrying, covenant couples "described their overall marital quality as better than did their standard counterparts. [C]ovenant couples were more committed to their marriage . . . whereas, their standard counterparts had changed little in their level of commitment." In addition, the follow-up surveys posited that:

> With the growing centrality of marriage for covenant couples, they experienced higher levels of commitment . . . , higher levels of agreement between partners . . . , fewer worries about having children . . . , and greater sharing of housework. It is not too early . . . to conclude that covenant marriages are better marriages. . . . Steven Nock, the director of the study, expresses the view that internally, the [covenant] marriages are vastly better, and covenant couples agree about who does what, the fairness of things, etc. much more than standard couples.

Not surprisingly, during hearings in the 2004 legislative session in Louisiana for the bill proposing six new provisions concerning covenant marriage content, Nock submitted commentary on each new provision and the extent to which those provisions "reflect[ed] many of the findings from" his research.

Marriage Transcends Individual Interest

Covenant couples are participating in a new form of marriage "that reserves the traditional, conventional, and religious aspects of the traditional institution, but also resolves the various inequities often associated with gender in modern marriages." In Nock's words, "a central theme that discriminates between the two types of unions . . . [is] institutionalization of the marriage." By institutionalization, Nock simply meant that the couple shares the view that

> the marriage warrants consideration apart from the individualistic concerns of either partner. In regard to some matters, covenant couples appear to defer to the interests of their marriage even when the individual concerns of the partners may appear to conflict. And this orientation to married life . . . helps resolve the customary problems faced by newly married couples in regard to fairness and equity.

By viewing marriage institutionally, covenant couples essentially "elevate the normative (expected) model of marriage to prominence in the relationship." One may, at this point, be pondering the following question:

> What accounts for this institutional view? The centrality accorded religion by the couple and beliefs about the life of marriage independently of the individual. Two individuals do not easily make a strong marriage. Rather, it takes the presence of a set of guiding principles around which these two individuals orient their behaviors and thinking.

Covenant couples, by their choice, seemingly offer themselves "collectively as witnesses to others about sacrificial love and its central role in binding male and female to each other and their offspring." Covenant couples, who already view marriage as a form of transcendent reality, reject post-modern marriage and its notion of a "loose union of two radically autonomous selves acting always in each person's own self-interest."

Viewpoint 

> *"[Covenant marriage] was a very hot idea that didn't catch on because not enough people wanted that choice."*

Covenant Marriage Won't Prevent Divorce for Most People

Don Monkerud

Don Monkerud argues in the following viewpoint that the covenant marriage movement will not affect more than a small percentage of persons. The movement, he argues, failed to win many adherents because it does not appeal to the average person. Monkerud says most states failed to adopt covenant marriage laws and in those state that have only a small percentage of those marrying enter into covenant marriages. Though still promoted by fundamentalist conservatives, he argues, it is doubtful that covenant marriage will have much influence on relationship patterns. Monkerud is a California-based writer who reports on cultural, social, and political issues.

As you read, consider the following questions:

1. According to research cited by the author, what percentage of those choosing covenant marriage are likely to be Baptist?

Don Monkerud, "Until the Death Penalty We Do Part . . . Covenant Marriage on the Rocks," *Counterpunch*, February 8, 2006. Reproduced by permission of the author.

2. What percentage of couples marrying in Arkansas entered into covenant marriages during the first three years it was legal to do so?
3. According to the author, state legislatures became interested in strengthening marriage because they thought divorce, cohabitation, and unmarried births caused an increase in what government budget expenditures?

After gaining media attention in the late 1990s with a promise to lower divorce rates across the nation, the Covenant Marriage Movement, heavily promoted by fundamentalist Christians, has hit the skids.

Putting God Back in Marriage

Growing out of earlier attempts to establish more permanent marriages, the "Covenant Marriage Movement" was founded in Dallas, Texas, by Phil and Cindy Waugh, a Baptist minister and his church-worker wife, in 1999. Today [2006] it has grown to 50,000 couples and 65 cooperating ministries. The Waughs claim marriage is not a contract or "simply an institution," and call on Christians to return to Biblical values that focus on marriage as "established by God and everlasting," based on acceptance of "God's intent for marriage and the importance of His presence in the marriage."

The Waughs see marriage as "under attack:" Divorce rates grew from 2.9 per 1,000 in 1968 to 4.2 per 1,000 in 1998 (they declined to 3.8 per 1,000 in 2002). Currently, the National Center for Health Statistics estimates that 40 percent of all marriages taking place right now will end in divorce.

For many, this call to return marriage to God's sphere makes sense. Many marriages occur in churches and include a variation of the vow: "I take thee to be my lawfully wedded spouse, to have and to hold from this day forward, for better or for worse, for richer or for poorer, in sickness and in health, 'til death do us part, according to God's holy ordinance and thereto I pledge thee my troth."

The Covenant Marriage Movement attempts to establish a special legal category of marriage that requires premarital counseling, signing a declaration of intent to live together "forever," disclosing personal history, and seeking counseling before divorce. Divorce is only allowed for infidelity, physical or sexual abuse, conviction of a felony or the death penalty, abandonment for one year, or living separately for two years. Irreconcilable differences are not grounds for divorce.

According to research from the Center for Family and Demographic Research at Bowling Green State University, religious factors are the largest, most dramatic indicators for those choosing covenant marriages. Those few who choose a covenant marriage are "significantly more likely to be Baptist (50 percent) or Protestant," and "differ greatly in religiosity and intensity of participation in religious activities."

Few States Adopt Covenant Marriage

Despite lobbying by church groups, only Arkansas, Arizona and Louisiana passed covenant marriage bills. Legislation was introduced but not passed in Iowa, Missouri, Indiana, Texas, Utah, Virginia, West Virginia, Mississippi, Oklahoma, South Carolina, Georgia, New Mexico, California, Kansas, Maryland, Minnesota, Oregon, Nebraska, Tennessee, Washington, and Florida.

On Valentine's Day 2005, Arkansas Governor Mike Huckabee, a Baptist minister turned conservative Republican, and his wife, took advantage of the Covenant Marriage Act of 2001 to convert their 30-year marriage to a covenant marriage in a ceremony in Little Rock. In February 2006, congregations across the South will participate in Covenant Marriage Sunday to reaffirm God's role in their marriages. But for the most part, the Covenant Marriage Movement failed to convince couples to make their marriages more difficult to escape.

Some 112,000 couples married in Arkansas in the first three years of the new law and only 800 of them, fewer than 1

Few Choose Covenant Marriage

The response [to covenant marriage] hasn't been what supporters hoped. Louisiana boasts the highest participation: about 1 in 50 new marriages, or 2 percent. In Arkansas, 600 couples have chosen covenant marriage in the last three years out of about 40,000 marriages a year. In Arizona, where a looser law allows couples a quick divorce if both spouses agree, participation is 1 percent.

About two dozen state legislatures have rejected covenant marriage laws since the late 1990s.

Eric Gorski,
"Covenant Marriages Aimed at Reducing Divorce Rates,"
Oakland Tribune, *February 27, 2005.*

percent, took advantage of the covenant marriage license. Fewer than 3 percent of couples in Louisiana and Arizona agreed to the extra restrictions of a covenant marriage. Following President [George W.] Bush's support of a Constitutional ban on gay marriage, proponents of covenant marriages attempted to reinvigorate the idea, but currently, no other states are expected to pass new marriage legislation.

Covenant Marriage Appeals to Small Group

"Covenant marriage just didn't take off," said Barbara Risman, cochair of the Council on Contemporary Families. "It was a very hot idea that didn't catch on because not enough people wanted that choice."

Risman views the Covenant Marriage Movement as more about religion than marriage, and a way to bring God more openly into traditional family values. She calls it "a wonderful idea" for individual rituals, although she doesn't think the state should play a role. Risman is not surprised at the push for covenant marriage in the South, "because it is the Bible Belt."

Steven Nock, director of the Marriage Matters project and a sociologist at the University of Virginia, describes covenant marriage as a reaction to "50 years of unstopped increases in divorce, unmarried births, and for the last 20 years, increases in cohabitation that went unnoticed by state and federal legislatures." When researchers pointed out high rates of poverty associated with single parent families, they invigorated religious conservatives and state legislatures to put a greater emphasis on marriage.

"At the moment, covenant marriage appeals to a small, distinct group who differ in important ways from the average person approaching marriage," said Nock. "Based on evidence we have at the moment, there is little to suggest that covenant marriage will soon appeal to a larger more diverse population."

Political Motivations for Covenant Marriage

In the 1950s, marriage and family were celebrated as the core of society, but religious conservatives became alarmed with social changes, which undermined the traditional family. Describing what they saw as decline and decadence, groups such as the Family Research Council and the Heritage Foundation reacted to the trends and began pushing a pro-family agenda in politics.

Nock explains that political interest in marriage also grew out of state legislatures becoming alarmed at increases in welfare and Medicare budgets and making a connection between divorce, cohabitation and unmarried births with low income and poverty. Before [President Bill] Clinton's welfare reforms in 1997 and 1998, only single women with children were allowed welfare; they were denied it if a man was present in the home, which led to the breakup of poor families. By reversing these trends, they hope to reduce welfare budgets.

"I doubt that government can predictably alter things like marriage and divorce," said Nock. "We are midway through a fundamental redefinition of what marriage is and are at the beginning of the reaction to that redefinition. Fifty years ago, marriage defined men and women's lives more than anything else, but it doesn't anymore."

Politicians No Longer Promote Covenant Marriage

Lowering welfare costs has replaced an emphasis on covenant marriage and become the primary justification for attempts by the Bush Administration to pass the Healthy Marriage Initiative, which would allot money to faith-based groups as part of a wider attempt to shore up marriage. Congress will take up the proposal in its new term.

When the Healthy Marriage Initiative didn't pass last term, the Bush Administration shifted federal funding into marriage initiative programs, such as a $583,475 grant from Health and Human Services (HHS) to the California Healthy Marriages Coalition. The money will finance an Internet resource center for California groups promoting marriage.

"We want to make marriage education widely accessible to everyone in every social economic stratum," said Dennis Stoicia, program director for the program. "Fifty percent of families that are not in poverty, end up in poverty after divorce. Frankly, marriage is a significant anti-poverty intervention."

Stoicia wouldn't make comments on gay or covenant marriage, which is outside the parameters of his grant, but the Orange County Marriage Resource Center Web site, which is a model for the California Healthy Marriages Coalition, reveals that a large portion of participants are religious.

The Covenant Marriage Movement is a failure, but promotion of marriage by fundamentalist conservatives and other religious groups is continuing. It's doubtful that the movement will have much influence on overall relationship patterns.

VIEWPOINT 3

"Poverty leads to divorce, not the other way around."

Reducing Poverty Can Prevent Divorce

Ailee Slater

Ailee Slater argues in the following viewpoint that poverty causes divorce. Money, she says, is one of the most prevalent causes of divorce. She claims that encouraging the poor to marry will likely lead to divorce because lack of money results in lack of a healthy marriage. The author contends that government spending on housing and employment opportunities for the impoverished—rather than marriage education—would reduce stress in marriages of low-income families. Slater writes for the Oregon Daily Emerald.

As you read, consider the following questions:

1. According to the author, what is the number one cause of arguments among married couples?
2. How, in the author's view, is divorce promoted when both parents are forced to work full time?
3. What will be the effect of programs that promote marriage without programs that also address poverty?

Congress wants to spend $100 million per year, for the next five years, to promote marriage, and marriage education. The federal funds will be directed toward low-income couples; the logic behind this plan being that if impoverished families can be swayed into getting married and staying married, those couples will need less monetary assistance later on in life. The plan also calls for $50 million per year to produce "committed fathers."

Organizations can apply for grants through the marriage program; for instance, one Fresno man of Marriage Mentoring Ministries Inc. has asked the government for $550,000 in order to hire more marriage counselors, trained to advise couples before and after marriage.

Marriage Education Isn't Enough

Low-income families do experience divorce far more frequently than those with higher income, and families headed by a single mother tend to be significantly poorer than two-parent families. Rep. Wally Herger of California, speaking in favor of funding the marriage promotion plan, noted that children growing up with only one parent are seven times more likely to grow up in poverty; Herger and others reason that if husband and wife can stay together, the entire family will be less likely to depend on monetary support from the government. Furthermore, because single mother households access welfare far more often than other families, the thinking goes that keeping marriages together will result in less need for welfare programs.

Offering marriage counseling, especially to families that might not be able to afford it on their own, will always be a good policy. However, the thinking behind the federal plan to promote marriage is slightly skewed, because poverty leads to divorce, not the other way around. Convincing low-income people to marry will not automatically raise their income; in fact, if both husband and wife are impoverished, and get mar-

Financial Problems Cause Divorce

[It is a] well known fact that money is often the root of marital problems. [According to Damon Carr,] "The divorce rate is an alarming 51%, meaning one out of every two marriages ends in divorce. Of those divorces, nearly 80% cited financial problems as the leading cause of the marital demise."

Dr. Bernice Wilson,
"Did Money Cause Us to Part: Divorce and Money,"
Metro News, *2007.*

ried, they probably will end up single because it seems to be that a lack of money results in the lack of a healthy marriage.

Money Causes Arguments

Marriage counselors, and national statistics, point out that money is the number one reason for arguments within a marriage, and one of the most prevalent causes of divorce. Impoverished couples struggle more than wealthy couples with meeting needs versus engaging in leisure activities; raising children; and spending time together as a family, because lower paying jobs mandate longer hours away from home. When both parents are forced to work full-time jobs, they have little time for bonding with each other, or their children, and it is therefore no surprise that divorce may ensue.

Therefore, if the federal government is serious about curbing our nation's high divorce rate, promoting more marriage—without a parallel promotion in programs that cater to low-income citizens in general—is extremely nearsighted.

In one example of how federal dollars to promote marriage have certainly gone awry, the aforementioned Marriage Mentoring Ministries Inc. organization spent a previous grant of $50,000 to hire a single employee, and create thousands of leaflets detailing the benefits of marriage.

No federal money should be wasted on pamphlets that attempt to convince citizens to tie the knot; couples unsure about a lifetime commitment to one another probably shouldn't get married, and we should hope that a leaflet would not convince them otherwise.

Low-Income Families Need Money

Furthermore, marriage does not need to be promoted as much as low-income families need simple monetary support. Were the federal government to pour money into revitalizing the housing and employment opportunities in impoverished neighborhoods, instead of flyers about marriage, couples would see a tangible reduction in the factors putting stress on their marriages.

As for the $50 million to sway fathers away from leaving their families, perhaps the government should consider investing a portion of that money in birth control services. Because many states offer limited access to birth control services, low-income citizens especially will have a more difficult time practicing safe sex; if a child is born to an unprepared couple, perhaps even a married one, that's the time when a father may choose to escape a familial commitment that he cannot handle financially or emotionally.

Poverty leads to single-parent households, yet being single in no way drives citizens toward being impoverished. It is laudable that congressional money be put toward counseling for low-income marriages, however, leaflets and other such programs that promote marriage, without programs addressing the problem of poverty in general, are simply useless.

VIEWPOINT 4

"The positive impact of premarital education on communication skills and marital satisfaction suggests it can reduce divorce rates."

Marriage Education Can Prevent Divorce

Alan J. Hawkins

Alan J. Hawkins argues in the following viewpoint that premarital education can strengthen marriage and thereby reduce divorce. Most marriages, he contends, break up because of lack of commitment, unrealistic expectations about marriage, and other factors that he says marriage education can address. Most people, he says, think marriage education is a good idea and would attend if the classes were available at no cost. The author asserts that marriage education improves relationship skills and marital quality, thus reducing the likelihood of divorce. Hawkins is a professor of family life at Brigham Young University.

As you read, consider the following questions:

1. What percentage of divorces result from marriages with low amounts of conflict, according to a study cited by the author?

2. According to a national study cited by the author, what percentage of unhappily married individuals are married to happily married individuals?
3. A survey cited by the author found that what percentage of ever-married respondents in Utah and Oklahoma thought formal preparation for marriage was a good idea?

Many legislators are wondering whether there is a constructive role that government can play to strengthen marriages and reduce divorces. A handful of states have passed legislation providing incentives for couples to participate in formal premarital education. The purpose of this article is to examine the research that can help answer the question whether legislation to promote premarital education can strengthen marriages and reduce the divorce rate. Of course, there are numerous legal and policy issues related to marriage and divorce being discussed these days. The focus of this article, however, is only on one. In the end, I conclude that legislation to promote premarital education is a feasible, cost-effective policy that is likely to strengthen marriages and reduce the divorce rate in states where it is implemented.

Existing Premarital Education Laws

Five states—Florida, Maryland, Minnesota, Oklahoma, and Tennessee—have passed legislation encouraging couples to participate in formal premarital education: education or counseling to help couples explore relationship strengths and weaknesses and learn what it takes to have a successful marriage. Other states, such as Utah, have considered this legislation but not acted upon or rejected it. The purpose of this legislation is to enhance the chances of couples achieving more stable, satisfying, and healthy marital relationships by encouraging the use of premarital education. The five statutes have minor differences but share much in common. Minnesota's statute requires twelve hours of education or counseling and specifies a minimum set of topics to cover. Other statutes generally require fewer hours of instruction or counseling; some are not as detailed about the content. All statutes allow for clergy members as well as secular educators or counselors to offer premarital education training. And couples who participate in marriage preparation in these five states can receive a discount on their marriage license fee. . . .

Premarital Education Can Address Reasons for Most Divorces

Even if one accepts the need to strengthen marriage and reduce divorce in our society, it does not necessarily follow that public policy and legislative initiatives can address the problem directly. Is it reasonable to think that some or many divorces can be prevented and, more specifically, could greater participation in premarital education help?

Certainly, many divorces are necessary to preserve the physical or psychological safety of an individual or to reinforce the moral boundaries of the institution of marriage. However, recent research suggests that most divorces are initiated because of "softer" personal or relationship problems, such as falling out of love, changing personal needs, lack of satisfaction, feelings of greater entitlement, and so forth. And this is especially true for more educated and well-off individuals. Another study of a representative sample of U.S. adults found that about two-thirds of divorces come from marriages with low amounts of conflict. This study also found that it was the children of divorce from low-conflict marriages who had the most challenged outcomes. The children of divorce who experienced volatile, high levels of conflict in their parents' marriage actually did better when their parents divorced compared to children whose parents had a volatile, high-conflict marriage but stayed married. In addition, one national study suggests that there are more "bad patches" in marriage than there are "bad marriages." This national study followed individuals who were unhappily married for several years and found that 60% of these individuals reported being happily married five years later, and another 20% reported significant improvement in marital satisfaction. These same researchers also reported that nearly 75% of unhappily married individuals were married to happily married partners. So usually at least one person in the marriage wants to keep it intact, and may want to work to improve the relationship in order to do so. Some divorces are in the best interests of the spouses and children involved. However, current research suggests that many divorces occur for reasons that can at least be addressed with effective premarital education.

Lack of Commitment

Other recent research also sheds light on the reasons for divorce. The NFI [National Fatherhood Initiative] marriage study asked divorced respondents to list major factors that contributed to their divorce. The most common reason given was "lack of commitment" (73%). Two state surveys with the identical question also found that lack of commitment was the most common reason given. Many reported that "too much arguing" (56%) and "infidelity" (55%) contributed to their divorce. "Marrying too young" (46%), "unrealistic expectations" (45%), and "lack of equality in the relationship" (44%) also were cited as major contributors to divorce. Twenty-nine percent listed "domestic violence" as a contributing factor. It is significant to note that 41% said a lack of premarital preparation contributed to their divorce.

Infidelity and Incompatibility

In another study, researchers content-analyzed open-ended responses to a similar question in a national sample. Their analysis suggested that women gave infidelity, incompatibility, and spouse's drinking/drug use as the three most common reasons for their divorce. Men reported incompatibility, infidelity, and lack of communication as the three most common reasons for their divorce.

Standard premarital education programs generally address most or all of the divorce factors listed above. Theoretically, then, legislation to promote premarital education would at least have the potential to strengthen marriages at their inception and reduce the chances of divorce. Again, however, it is important to recognize that preventing *all* divorces is not good public policy. As these data suggest, some divorces need to occur to preserve physical or psychological safety and to reinforce the moral boundaries of marriage. . . .

Americans Favor Premarital Education

How many couples participate in formal premarital education before marrying? And do people think marriage preparation is a good idea? According to the NFI marriage study, about 37% of ever-married adults in the United States have participated in formal marriage preparation. Surveys in six different states (California, Florida, Oklahoma, New York, Texas, Utah) put this figure between 27% (Utah) and 38.5% (Texas), with couples spending a range of ten to fifteen hours in formal instruction. Of those couples who participated in formal education, a large majority did so in religious settings. It should be noted, however, that some survey respondents' notions of premarital education would likely include activities or programs that lasted for only a few hours. Moreover, the content and quality of these programs could vary considerably.

Recent surveys suggest that most Americans think formal preparation for marriage is a good idea, regardless of their involvement in it. In both the Oklahoma and Utah surveys, more than 90% of ever-married respondents said that formal marriage preparation was important. Also, several state surveys asked whether unmarried individuals would be interested in participating in formal premarital education. Most respondents, ranging from 68% (in Oklahoma and Utah) to 81% (in California), reported that they would be interested in formal premarital education. Two of these surveys (the Oklahoma and Utah surveys) broke down this response by income level and found somewhat higher interest in premarital education among lower-income individuals and those receiving public assistance.

In the NFI marriage study, respondents were asked if they would attend premarital education classes if they were made available at no cost; 73% said yes. In a related question, 86% of American adults agreed that "all couples considering marriage should be encouraged to get premarital counseling." The six state surveys asked, "Is a statewide/government initiative to promote healthy marriages and reduce the number of divorces in the state a good idea?" Most agreed with this statement (from 62% in New York to 87% in Utah). Accordingly, these data suggest that a strong majority of Americans believe in the importance of formal premarital education and would likely be supportive of public policy efforts to encourage it.

Modern Marriage Requires Skills

Some may wonder about the value of premarital education. Some may believe that marriage is something that we can only learn as we go along, or that it comes naturally. Arguably, a few generations ago, marriage involved more prescribed roles and responsibilities, lower expectations for personal fulfillment, stronger support systems, stronger beliefs in permanence, and higher barriers to ending a relationship. In these circumstances, perhaps a "learn-as-you-go" approach to marriage was more feasible. Or if this "learn-as-you-go" approach was not particularly effective, at least the risk of divorce was still low. Today, however, marital roles for most are as negotiated as they are prescribed, marriage carries high expectations for personal fulfillment, marriage is a more private institution with fewer social and cultural supports, the belief in marital permanence has eroded, and barriers to ending a marriage are much lower than in the past due to unilateral, no-fault divorce laws and women's greater economic independence. Accordingly, compared to the past, there is an increasing need for greater knowledge and relationship skills for contemporary marriages to succeed. And because the highest risk for divorce occurs during the first five years of marriage, early education seems to make sense.

Cohabitation Doesn't Teach Marriage Skills

In addition, there is a modern version of the "learn-as-you-go" approach to marriage. About five million individuals are cohabiting in the United States, and most young people today (66% of boys and 61% of girls) believe that living together before marriage is a good way to increase the chances of a successful marriage. Even in more conservative areas, such as Utah and Oklahoma, more than a third of young people (ages eighteen to twenty-four) believe that cohabitation will improve their chances of a successful marriage. In short, some youth approaching marriage may dismiss the need for formal premarital education because they believe that cohabitation is the best way to prepare effectively for a good marriage. However, scientific evidence shows that cohabitation is a substantial risk factor for later divorce unless one cohabits with only one partner and eventually marries that partner, which is not the norm. Moreover, research suggests that those who cohabit before marrying have poorer marital quality than those who do not cohabit, even controlling for various selection effects. No research to date suggests that cohabitation is an effective means for enhancing marital success. Accordingly, the dramatic rise of cohabitation has not decreased the need for formal premarital education in our society. Instead, it has probably increased the need. Cohabiting couples should benefit from premarital education as well.

Premarital Education Creates "Reality Check"

The dominant cultural belief about marriage, one consistently portrayed in the entertainment media, is that individuals search and finally find their one-and-only soul mate, fall deeply and effortlessly in love, and marriage is simply the public avowal of that love. Relatively few cultural messages reinforce the reality that marriage takes knowledge, skills, and commitment to make it work. Thus, premarital education is an important way that engaged couples are given a reality check and invited to learn skills that will help them build a truer soul-mate relationship. In the process they are likely to understand that the quality and success of a marriage depends largely on attitudes and action rather than love and luck.

Utah Commission on Marriage, "Does Legislation to Encourage Formal Premarital Education Make Sense for Utah?" June 2005.

Education Improves Relationship Skills

Formal marriage preparation may make sense, and Americans may believe it is a good idea for themselves and everyone else. But is there scientific evidence that formal premarital education can achieve its goal of helping couples form and sustain healthy marriages? And does it have the ability to reduce divorce? The evidence on this question is not yet definitive. But an increasing body of research suggests that the answer to these questions is yes.

A synthesis of studies (meta-analysis) evaluating the outcomes of formal marriage preparation found evidence supporting the effectiveness of these programs. Of the thirteen most rigorous studies, twelve found that couples who participated in premarital education programs had significantly higher relationship skills and marital quality after the program compared to couples who did not participate. The researchers found that the average person who participated in a premarital prevention program was better off after the program than 79% of the control-group couples who did not receive premarital education. Similarly, premarital program participants had a 69% chance of improving their relationship quality compared to only a 31% chance of improvement for nonparticipants. In the seven studies that included follow-up evaluations six months to three years after the end of these premarital programs, program participants generally maintained the relationship skills they were taught, including effective conflict negotiation, positive communication, empathy, and self-disclosure. In addition, a recent comprehensive meta-analysis of the effectiveness of all different kinds of marriage education programs also found that marriage education for engaged couples was effective.

These researchers note, however, that the studies were almost uniformly done with white, middle-class samples. Clearly, more research is needed to assess the effectiveness of premarital education for more disadvantaged populations. Two large-scale research projects funded by the federal government are underway that will be able to investigate this question with unmarried, new-parent, fragile family couples and lower-income engaged couples. Generally, more at-risk groups have more to gain from effective intervention, but this will need to be shown empirically.

Education Reduces Separation and Divorce

In another recent study, researchers following a representative sample of newlywed couples in Louisiana for five years found that couples who sought out premarital education had a substantially lower rate of separation and divorce in the early years of marriage, even controlling for a host of other factors that could influence the likelihood of divorce. Another bit of accumulating evidence for the value of formal premarital education comes from a recent evaluation of Community Marriage Policies (CMPs) in the United States. In CMP communities, religious leaders have banded together to strengthen marriages and reduce divorce. There are more than 200 communities in the United States that have signed CMPs. The primary feature of these community coalitions is that the religious organizations agree to require couples seeking a religious wedding to undergo extensive premarital education. Researchers found that CMP communities reduced their divorce rates 2% more than comparable communities. Although the additional 2% decline in divorce may not seem impressive, researchers estimated that, on a national level, these policies reduced the number of divorces by more than 30,000 since being implemented.

Education Improves Marital Quality

In addition, data from state surveys provide some support for the notion that premarital education can make a positive difference in marital quality. Of Utahns who said they participated in formal premarital education, 84% reported that they were "very happy" in their marriages compared to 71% who did not participate in formal premarital education. Those who participated in formal premarital education also reported higher scores on talking to each other as friends, lower negative interaction scores, and lower divorce proneness scores. Similar results were found in surveys of representative samples of adults in other states; large majorities of those who participated in formal marriage preparation said it positively affected their relationship. Similarly, a recent study of adults in several states also found that those who participated in premarital education had higher marital satisfaction and commitment than those who did not participate. In addition, those who participated in premarital education reported less marital conflict. Finally, premarital education was associated with a 31% decline in the odds of divorce.

Education Can Reduce Divorce

For individuals who were not involved in premarital education, the probability of divorce within the first five years of marriage was significantly higher than for those who had been involved in premarital education, although this finding applied primarily to individuals with higher levels of education. Again, there could be other differences between those who participated in premarital education and those who did not that could account for the differences in outcomes studied, but the researchers attempted to control statistically for many of these possible differences.

In summary, there is mounting scientific evidence that participation in formal premarital education makes a positive difference in subsequent marital quality, at least in the early, higher-risk years of marriage. More research is needed to examine whether participation in premarital education reduces the risk of divorce. The research on this important question is limited and inconclusive, although the positive impact of premarital education on communication skills and marital satisfaction suggests it can reduce divorce rates.

VIEWPOINT 5

> *"The Surrendered Wife movement . . . has saved my marriage."*

Surrendered Wives Movement Can Prevent Divorce

Amanda Cable

Amanda Cable argues in the following viewpoint that women in the Surrendered Wives movement (SWM) believe that obedience to the husband can save marriage. SWM proponents assert that relinquishing control to the husband allows a wife to release the habit of nagging and arguing. They maintain that this practice restores harmony. Wives, members of the movement argue, should never criticize husbands or attempt to "remake" them. Though obedience goes against conventional notions of equality, SWM proponents claim it restores intimacy. Cable writes for The Daily Mail *in London, England.*

As you read, consider the following questions:

1. As related by the author, what was the first visualization lesson in surrendering given by the Surrendered Wives tutor?
2. As related by the author, what instructions do Surrendered Wives receive regarding sex?

Amanda Cable, "I Became a Stepford Wife and Saved My Marriage," *Daily Mail*, May 3, 2007. Reproduced by permission.

3. Based upon the experiences of the woman used to illustrate this viewpoint, how would becoming a Surrendered Wife affect the amount of housework the wife does?

The scene was so highly charged it looked set to ignite another explosive domestic row. There, her eyes smouldering with adolescent rebellion, stood a teenage daughter, next to her was her fiercely protective mother and, facing the pair, the girl's stepfather, who was attempting to admonish her for defying his will.

As Ali Tavassoli finished his scolding, he braced himself for the reaction he'd become all too used to over many years from his shrewish wife, who had always resisted his attempts to discipline her daughter, feeling that only she should take on that role of parental enforcer.

Yet instead of the expected belligerence, she hesitated and gulped before saying a little robotically: 'Ali, you are a sensible and intelligent man. I love you and it is my role in life to support you.' If it is hard to believe that a woman with her character could be quite so subservient, the shock to her family was even greater. Both husband and daughter burst into tears of surprise.

Relinquishing Control

Karen recalls: 'I think that was the moment I truly became a surrendered housewife—and actually saved my marriage in the process. I was stunned by my own reaction because I've been arguing and bickering with and nagging Ali nonstop for nine years.

'But I didn't actually realise just how much my behaviour had affected the whole family until I gave in to Ali for the first time, and both he and Yasmin started to cry because they were so happy and relieved.' Given that until a few weeks earlier the house had been a battleground, Karen's extraordinary capitulation must have seemed too good to be true for her long-suffering husband.

The story of how this sharp-tongued working wife and mother from Leeds agreed to relinquish all control to her husband—swopping furious rows for sweet acquiescence in a bid to win back his affections—is the subject of a new Channel Five documentary, *Obedient Wives.*

The idea of the Surrendered Wife comes from a book by American Laura Doyle—a former marketing copywriter whose opinions make Ma Walton look like a feminist activist.

A Movement to Surrender

It has spawned a whole Surrendered Wives movement which goes far beyond the wildest dreams of your average Stepford Wife. Devotees agree to relinquish all control of their husband's life, allowing him to make all the decisions, never saying 'no' to sex, and finally learning to change themselves and not their men.

The idea is that men can't change—so women are the ones who need a radical rethink in order to preserve romance in marriages.

Surrendered Wives even have their own Web site, complete with images of red roses and sugar-coated assurances from Laura Doyle that 'none of us feels good about ourselves when we're nagging, critical or controlling.

'Through surrendering, you will find the courage to gradually stop indulging in these unpleasant behaviours and replace them with dignified ones.' In a conciliatory tone liable to make feminists froth at the mouth, she urges followers to ask: 'Which do I want more: to have control of every situation or to have an intimate marriage?' But is there any substance to these claims? Could they actually make any difference to a modern-day marriage being torn apart at the seams by arguments?

Trying to Remake the Husband

Enter Karen, a 39-year-old mother of two and successful business manager, who admits to a lifetime of bossy behaviour.

She says: 'My father was a mild-mannered mechanic, and my mother was a stay-at-home housewife.

'She ran her home and five children with military-style precision, and took every decision there was about the house and money.

'She controlled Dad utterly, and even as a child I subconsciously copied her, always striving to be in control of any situation. In my 20s, I had a brief, unhappy marriage with a very dominant husband.

'It nearly destroyed me, and when we split up I found myself single with a two-year-old daughter, Yasmin. I vowed that no man would ever get the chance to dominate me again.

'I met Ali, a courier, soon afterwards.

'We bumped into each other when we were shopping, started talking outside and quickly fell in love. He is naturally gentle and romantic, while I am ambitious and strive for perfection.

'When we married nine years ago, I started to try to mould Ali into a perfect husband. Somehow, without me realising it, my attempts to change him turned into a hamster-wheel of nonstop criticism, nagging and inevitable arguments. Ali just couldn't seem to do anything right. If he expressed an opinion, I would immediately disagree and argue until I got my own way. I didn't trust him to do anything around the house, so I would come home from work tired and stressed, and start to cook and control the family.

'The worst conflict was when Ali tried to discipline the children. Our son Kia is three, and if Ali told him off I would often accuse him of being too harsh.

'But if Ali dared to tell Yasmin off, I would immediately leap to her defence, even if she was in the wrong.

'Each time, it would lead to an explosive row between Ali and me, while Yasmin would sneak off and her misdemeanour would be long forgotten.' By last November [2006], as documentary makers were hunting for a real-life shrew for their television taming, Karen's marriage had hit crisis point.

Becoming a Nag

She says: 'I was in utter despair. My controlling became worse after I was promoted at work, becoming a manager with a team of staff working for me. I was so used to giving out orders that I would simply come home and treat Ali in exactly the same way.

'If he dared to try to defend himself, I would simply explode, and yet another row would erupt. We were rowing every single evening—almost every hour.

'I started to dread weekends because even a trip to the supermarket would end in a huge disagreement. Ali couldn't pick something from the shelf without me telling him to use another brand.

'Inside, I was desperately unhappy and insecure. I was terrified of losing him, but I couldn't stop the way I was.

'After one particularly vicious weekend of rowing, I sat down and looked at our wedding pictures.

'We looked so happy and carefree, and I couldn't believe the difference between the smiling bride and the nagging old hag I had become.' That week, Karen saw an advertisement asking for volunteers for a television programme.

Lessons in Surrender

She says: 'It came through on the e-mail at the call centre where I work, and when I saw the words "Is your marriage in crisis?" I started to read. It explained briefly about Surrendered Wives, and gave a telephone number.

'I didn't like the term surrender because it sounded like just giving in, but I was absolutely desperate and prepared to try anything to save my marriage.' Karen was given two days of training by Surrendered Wives tutor Ellen Hale, a woman who (taking a stance that will infuriate many modern women) readily blames working wives for lack of marital harmony.

Ellen says: 'More and more women are working, becoming CEOs of companies and gaining status in the work world. It is very hard for them to come home and be a feminine person and a wife, and be loving and soft and caring—they just come home with this boss attitude instead.' For her first lesson in Surrendering, Ellen handed an astounded Karen a roll of gaffer tape 'to help her visualise her own mouth being taped shut'.

Karen says: 'Whenever I was about to disagree with Ali, or to try and boss him, I had to imagine tape over my mouth to keep me from saying anything'.

Karen was asked to take Ali and their son Kia to the hairdresser's—giving Ali the say on how everyone's new style should look.

Watching with a look of sheer agony as her husband chose his own haircut for the first time in nearly a decade, she allowed him to arrange Kia's haircut, too.

Finally, it was time for her own—and she sat horrified in the chair while Ali cheerfully asked the stylist to 'curl' his wife's hair. 'He's so old fashioned—he wants me to look like [actress] Farrah Fawcett,' she hissed.

But Surrendered Wives allow their husbands to choose how they should look—and an hour later, as Karen inspected her new 'poodle' look in front of the mirror, she forced herself through gritted teeth to smile and congratulate Ali on his wise choice.

Praise, Gratitude and Apologies

She recalls: 'It was hard to lavish him with praise all the time, because I simply hadn't ever done it before.

'He thought I was actually joking when I first started to compliment him.

Give Up Control

If you can admit that you frequently or sometimes control, nag, or criticize your husband, then it is up to you and you alone to take the actions described here to restore intimacy to your marriage and dignity and peace to yourself.

I am not saying that you are responsible for every problem in your marriage. You are not. Your husband has plenty of areas he could improve too, but that's nothing you can control. You can't make him change—you can only change yourself. The good news is that since you've identified the behaviors that contribute to your problems, you can begin to solve them. Rather than wasting time thinking about what my husband should do, I prefer to keep all my energy for improving my happiness. The point of my journey was to give up controlling behavior, and to look inward instead of outward.

I encourage you to do the same.

You won't have to look far for someone to tell you that surrendering is crazy, but it isn't. It's not crazy to want romance and passion in your marriage. It's not crazy to want to feel respect for your life partner. It's not crazy to give up doing things that deplete your spirit and ask for help. It's not crazy to stop trying to control things you have no control over. It is scary, but it's not crazy. Don't let people who lack your courage tell you otherwise.

Laura Doyle, "The Surrendered Wife,"
2005. www.surrenderedwife.com.

But praise and gratitude are two essential parts of the Surrendered Wife training.' So, too, is apology. Ali, 38, recalls: 'After a few days, Karen sat me down and said "I'm really sorry because sometimes I'm really disrespectful to you. I apologise and I won't let it happen again". I honestly thought she was delirious—I was so shocked that I couldn't speak.

'Karen had never apologised once.

'But, suddenly, she was meekly saying sorry for the way she'd behaved in the past!' By now, Karen was in full surrender mode—and next came the end to the explosive arguments.

She says: 'I learned to agree with Ali, to smile and say that he was an intelligent man whose decisions I respected. If he had an outrageous plan, like a hideous new colour scheme for the living room—I knew I wasn't allowed to erupt.

'Of course, it was hard at times not to give him both barrels but I felt that, if I was going to go through with this, I'd have to stick to it.

'Instead, I would pause and say "That sounds really interesting. Also, what about doing it this way as well—would you consider this idea?"

Never Refuse Sex

Surrendered wives are not allowed to say "but" or be too negative. If your husband is clearly wrong, you can try to patiently offer him another alternative, while never criticising what he has said.' If such verbal surrender was just about bearable, Karen struggled rather more with the thorniest element of her new role—sex.

As Ellen outlined this aspect of the challenge, Karen found herself bridling at the instruction 'never refuse your husband sex'.

She says: 'I was told to make myself available for lovemaking at least once a week.' She pauses, and adds: 'I don't like lying back and thinking of England—my marriage was in such crisis that we weren't even kissing and cuddling.

'But this was the area that surprised me most. Acting like a Surrendered Wife physically, cuddling him and putting my hand on his knee, have helped bring an easy intimacy that we had lost.

'If Ali does say anything that is hurtful to me I can't hit back with a witty and well-timed riposte like I always used to in the past. Instead, I look hurt and just say: "Ouch. Ali, what you said really did hurt me."

'He immediately looks really sorry and puts his arm around me—and it diffuses a situation which would have ended in a row.' So what difference has two months of being a Surrendered Wife made to the Tavassoli marriage? Karen says: 'I have been raised as an independent woman and the Surrendered Wife movement goes against everything I've stood for.

Surrender Saves Marriage

'But, incredibly, it has saved my marriage. I don't do more housework—I do less, because Ali is so amazed to be thanked so nicely for every small thing he does that he has started loading the dishwasher for the first time in years.

'Before, I would just have criticised him for putting the dishes in the wrong way. He is so thrilled with the "New" Karen that he even told me to sit and watch a film the other night so he could do the ironing.

'He appreciates there is a closeness between us that we had lost.' Ali himself—a husband so henpecked he still bears mental scars—agrees his wife's change of character altered the dynamics of their marriage dramatically.

Putting his arm around his wife's shoulders and giving her a hefty squeeze, he smiles and says: 'I like the fact that she has surrendered. I know it was hard for her—nagging is a bit like an addiction.

'But we were so unhappy before, and the rows were terrible. Now she smiles sweetly and asks me what I think about everything. We don't row, we just cuddle like teenagers—and it is wonderful.'

> *"I cannot understand how an independent, educated woman would want to hostage herself to such a lopsided reliance on someone else's benevolence."*

Surrendered Wives Movement Demeans Women

Ceri Radford

Ceri Radford argues in the following viewpoint that the Surrendered Wives movement is demeaning to women. Complete reliance upon the husband's decision in all matters is, she argues, the equivalent to being a hostage. The idea that a woman should never say no to sex, she says, demeans both the husband and the wife. The author contends that Surrendered Wives abandon responsibility for their own lives. To defer to the husband in all matters, she asserts, systematically removes a woman's confidence in her own judgment. Radford blogs for the Web site http://blogs.telegraph.co.uk.

As you read, consider the following questions:

1. As recited by the author, what did the Surrendered Wife who was the breadwinner in the family have to do before spending money to purchase anything?

Ceri Radford, "'Surrendered Wives'; Make Me Squirm," Telegraph.co.uk, May 8, 2007. Reproduced by permission.

2. The author describes a Surrendered Wife who teaches her daughter that they sweep the floor "to honor Daddy." In the view of the author, what would have been a more sensible explanation?
3. How, in the author's view, does removing a woman's self-confidence in her own judgment affect the ability of women to get out of an abusive, alcoholic, or adulterous relationship?

Last night I saw something on TV that made me so simultaneously cross and queasy that I'm going to have to abandon books for the moment and blog about it.

Channel 5's 'secret lives' series ran a programme on 'obedient wives': women who have decided that all this sexual equality business is bunkum and what they really need to do to ensure marital bliss is to surrender total control of their lives to their husbands.

Unsurprisingly perhaps, this fad comes from the US: launched by Laura Doyle in her book *The Surrendered Wife* and fanned by the gentle breezes of ardent Christianity.

The Channel 5 programme revealed some of the faces behind the philosophy, for want of a more appropriate word. There was learner 'surrenderer' Karen from Leeds, who snipped up her credit cards and has to ask her husband's permission to buy anything even though she is the breadwinner of the family.

Sweeping the Floor to Honor Daddy

And Crystal, the 24-year-old home school graduate from the States, shown doing the housework with her two-year-old daughter and chanting: 'Why are we sweeping the floor? To honour Daddy!' 'Why are we making this fruit pizza? To honour Daddy!' Isn't a clean floor just nice and hygienic in its own right? And is there a possible satisfactory answer to the second question?

Surrendered Wives Are Just Dolls

If a man wants that sort of relationship, he actually doesn't want a relationship, he wants a doll. He wants a puppet, he wants total control and that's not the definition of a relationship but if she has chosen to do that to please him, then, in their heads, maybe they have a relationship, that his idea of relationship is total control and her idea of relationship is total submission.

Pru Goward, Australian member of Parliament,
60 Minutes, *Australia, June 3, 2007.*

Then there was another young American mum, whose name evades me, pictured covering her face with fear as she watched her young son being driven round the garden by his Dad on a motorbike. She seemed to think it was dangerous, but who was she to complain? It was up to her husband to judge, weak, feckless female that she is.

To be fair to the women involved, I'm sure the documentary presented as hammy and provocative a view as possible of their beliefs. And whether or not this is borne out in the long-term reality, they all said surrendering had made them happy.

Freed from the shackles of actually taking responsibility for their own lives, they discovered marital harmony, romance, femininity, and . . . an eerie addiction to photos of flowers and curlicue fonts.

Simpler Not to Assert Your Own View

I can sort of understand the appeal. Religious arguments aside, I'm sure surrendering cuts squabbling: far simpler to go along with everything your husband says rather than to assert your own view or negotiate something as sophisticated as a compromise.

And if you are going to dedicate yourself to your husband's domestic comforts on top of your own job, like any good surrendered wife, he may well feel magnanimous enough to treat you to the odd slap-up meal out in return for your skivvying.

I suppose there's also the more academic argument that our perceptions of strength and weakness are culturally subjective: modern western society may have championed the empowerment of women, others see passivity and acceptance as the hallmarks of female strength.

It reminds me of Chaucer's *The Clerk's Tale*, which paints a picture of the perfect wife as someone who wouldn't stoop to complaining even when her husband took her two children away in turn to be killed. The conclusion revealed that it was all a ruse: the children were in fact kept safe, while the husband was just exploring the forbearance of his wife—who passed this grisly test with flying, if not feminist, colours.

OK, it's a bit of a leap, but you can see the parallels with surrendered wives.

Resentment and Dependence

If you are bound to a code that prohibits complaining or questioning your husband's authority, how unreasonable does he have to be before you rebel? Does buying a mini motorbike for a six-year-old count? Or a flame-thrower? What if there's an accident? Recriminations are out of the question. How will you deal with the resentment?

The 'Surrendered Wife' movement may make it clear that 'remaining in an abusive, alcoholic, or adulterous relationship is not promoted or condoned,' but if you have systematically removed a woman's confidence in her own judgement, how do you expect her to act decisively if a marriage teeters towards any of these states?

If your husband is fair-minded, kind and consistent, the ideas may well boost a flagging relationship. But I cannot understand how an independent, educated woman would want to hostage herself to such a lopsided reliance on someone else's benevolence. And as for Laura Doyle's other lovely tenet that a wife should never say no to sex—how is this not reductive and demeaning to both parties?

Surrender Is Pernicious

Maybe it's not worth getting wound up about. Some people choose to live according to moral codes I find frankly creepy and bizarre: so what? There are worse things going on out there than a woman in Leeds letting her husband tell the hairdresser to curl her hair when she prefers it straight.

But I still can't help feeling that this lighthearted look at women who surrender themselves up to their husband, their God, or a nebulous combination of the two taps into something a lot more pernicious. Without wanting to imply a moral equivalence, there are shades of Ayaan Hirsi Ali's definition of submission—that a Muslim wife should accept without question whatever she is subjected to, whatever the personal suffering.

The emancipation of women may have thrown up some genuinely difficult questions about marriage, child care, work and life balance, but I'm pretty sure the solution isn't to surrender.

Periodical Bibliography

The following articles have been selected to supplement the diverse views presented in this chapter.

Stephanie Coontz — "The Origins of Modern Divorce," *Family Process*, March 1, 2007.

Don Dinkmeyer Jr. — "A Systematic Approach to Marriage Education," *Journal of Individual Psychology*, vol. 63, no.3, Fall 2007.

Cynthia Hanson — "Can This Marriage Be Saved?" *Ladies' Home Journal*, vol. 125, no. 1, January 2008.

Sharyl Jupe and Jann Blackstone-Ford — "Forgiveness May Help Save Marriage," *Contra Costa Times* (Walnut Creek, CA), August 15, 2006.

Tim Luckhurst — "No, Let's Not Make Divorce Any Easier: Institution of Marriage Is in Enough Trouble Already," *The Daily Mail*, May 26, 2006.

Randy Mascagni — "Money Matters an Important Consideration in Divorce," *Mississippi Business Journal*, October 16, 2006.

Robyn Parker — "The Effectiveness of Marriage and Relationship Education Programs," *Family Matters*, no. 77, Spring 2008.

Viola Polomeno — "Marriage, Parenthood, and Divorce: Understanding the Past as We Move into the Future," *International Journal of Childbirth Education*, June 1, 2007.

Karen Uhlenhuth — "Healthy Families' Program Aims to Help Couples Emotionally, Economically," *The Kansas City Star* (MO), January 14, 2008.

Julie Ward — "Covenant Marriage in Comparative Perspective," *Theological Studies*, vol. 67, no. 4, December 2006.

Lee Williams — "Premarital Counseling," *Journal of Couple & Relationship Therapy*, vol.6, no. 1/2, 2007.

Chapter 3

Do Divorce Laws Work?

Chapter Preface

Marriage is a legal status and divorce is the legal process for ending that status. Laws concerning divorce address not only whether divorce is permitted, but also other important issues concerning property, support, and custody of children.

Prior to the 1970s, divorce could be granted only if grounds for the divorce existed, such as adultery or abuse. Because many people wanted to be divorced but had not committed acts of adultery or abuse, parties often fabricated acts of adultery or cruelty so that a court would grant a divorce. This meant that parties routinely committed perjury in order to dissolve their marriages. This dismayed legal commentators as it undermined the integrity of the legal system, many of whom argued that persons who wished to be divorced should not have to choose between living in an unhappy marriage or lying in court.

In 1970, California adopted the first "no-fault" divorce statute, providing that the only grounds required for a divorce were "irreconcilable differences." Other states followed suit. Today, all states except New York have adopted "no-fault" divorce. Sociologists Michele Adams and Scott Coltrane have observed that no-fault divorce "changed divorce from an adversarial system pitting victims against victimizers, with the state acting as enforcer of marital norms, to a private decision between unhappily married but legally blameless partners."

A 2004 study by Justin Wolfers and Betsey Stephenson found that suicide rates for women and domestic violence rates dropped after states adopted no-fault divorce. In explanation of the correlation between these positive trends and the change in divorce laws, Wolfers says that no-fault divorce "may actually provide a safety valve for the pressures of family life."

Some blame what they see as the breakdown of the family, however, on the ease of no-fault divorce. Katherine Spaht, a law professor at Louisiana State University, has observed that "[e]asy divorce that makes for an 'easy' exit communicates society's view that it has little interest in the lasting commitment of two people to love and care for each other and to bear and rear the next generation." Critics of no-fault divorce also often cite the effect of divorce on children. According to economist Douglas W. Allen, "the real negative impact of the no-fault divorce regime was on children, and increasing the divorce rate meant increasing numbers of disadvantaged children."

Historically, women have been primary caretakers of children and men have been primary breadwinners. Changing gender roles and the notion of equality of gender during the past few decades, however, has promoted increased involvement of fathers in the care of children both during the marriage and after a divorce. Most states have a presumption or preference in favor of joint custody. Proponents of joint custody argue that it promotes a continuing and substantial relationship between the child and both parents, albeit in separate households. Opponents of joint custody argue that trying to be part of two households can be confusing and stressful for a child.

Although there are currently around 2.3 million single fathers, the 2002 U.S. Census found that 85 percent of custodial parents were mothers. Some fathers claim that this is just one example of how divorce laws are unfair to men. A number of groups exist to promote fathers' rights and seek more even-handed treatment of men and women in divorce.

VIEWPOINT 1

"To do justice between parties without regard to fault is an impossibility."

No-Fault Divorce Is Harmful

Stephen Baskerville

Stephen Baskerville argues in the following viewpoint that no-fault divorce rewards wrongdoers. Marriage is a contract, he argues, and no-fault divorce allows a party to break the contract without consequences. Divorce, he says, usually has a more detrimental effect on children than high-conflict marriages. The author contends that no-fault divorce often deprives the innocent spouse access to his or her children. Requiring fault for divorce, he argues, will be more just and will deter unnecessary divorces. Baskerville is a political scientist at Howard University.

As you read, consider the following questions:

1. According to the author, what group was the "ideological machine" that promoted no-fault divorce?
2. According to a *Time*/CNN poll quoted by the author, what percentage of Americans think it should be harder for couples with small children to divorce?

Stephen Baskerville, "The No-Blame Game: Why No-Fault Divorce is Our Most Dangerous Social Experiment," *Crisis*, vol. 23, March 2005, pp. 14–20.

3. What percentage of children experienced relief when their parents divorced, according to a study cited by the author?

While lamenting the high divorce rate is conventional piety among family advocates, most have refused to challenge the divorce laws. The standard rationalization is that to control divorce we must first change the culture. But no one suggests that changing the culture is a prerequisite for preventing, say, abortion. While cultural forces certainly contribute, the divorce epidemic has proceeded directly from a legal system which permits and even encourages it.

No-Fault Rewards Wrongdoers

No-fault divorce laws were introduced in the United States and other industrialized countries during the 1970s and are being expanded into other regions of the world today. "No-fault" is a misnomer (taken from car insurance), for the new laws did not stop at removing the requirement that grounds be cited for a divorce. But they did create unilateral and involuntary divorce, so that one spouse may end a marriage without any agreement or fault by the other. Moreover, the spouse who divorces or otherwise abrogates the marriage contract incurs no liability for the costs or consequences, creating a unique and unprecedented legal anomaly. "In all other areas of contract law those who break a contract are expected to compensate their partner," writes Robert Whelan of London's Institute of Economic Affairs, "but under a system of 'no-fault' divorce, this essential element of contract law is abrogated."

In fact, the legal implications go farther, since the courts actively assist the violator. Attorney Steven Varnis points out that "the law generally supports the spouse seeking the divorce, even if that spouse was the wrongdoer." "No-fault" did not really remove fault, therefore; it simply allowed judges to redefine it however they pleased. It introduced the novel concept that one could be deemed guilty of violating an agreement that one had, in fact, not violated. "According to therapeutic precepts, the fault for marital breakup must be shared, even when one spouse unilaterally seeks a divorce," observes Barbara Whitehead in *The Divorce Culture*. "Many husbands and wives who did not seek or want divorce were stunned to learn that they were equally 'at fault' in the dissolution of their marriages."

No Binding Agreements to Create Family

The "fault" that was ostensibly thrown out the front door of divorce proceedings re-entered through the back, but now with no precise definition. The judiciary was expanded from its traditional role of punishing crime or tort to punishing personal imperfections and private differences: One could now be summoned to court without having committed any infraction; the verdict was pre-determined; and one could be found "guilty" of things that were not illegal. Lawmakers created an "automatic outcome," writes Judy Parejko, author of *Stolen Vows*. "A defendant is automatically found 'guilty' of irreconcilable differences and is not allowed a defense."

Though marriage ostensibly falls under civil law, the logic quickly extended into the criminal. The "automatic outcome" expanded into what effectively became a presumption of guilt against the involuntarily divorced spouse (the defendant). Yet the due process protections of formal criminal proceedings did not apply, so involuntary divorcees could become criminals without any action on their part and in ways they were powerless to avoid. In some jurisdictions, a divorce defendant is the only party in the courtroom without legal immunity.

Contrary to the assumptions of "change the culture" thinking, these laws were not enacted in response to public demand: No popular clamor to dispense with divorce restrictions preceded their passage; no public outrage at any perceived injustice provided the impetus; no public debate was ever held in the media. Legislators "were not responding to widespread public pressure but rather acceding to the well-orchestrated lobbying of a few activists," writes Christensen. "Eclipsed in the media by other issues—such as civil rights, Vietnam, Watergate, and abortion"—the new laws rapidly swept the nation "with little publicity and no mass support."

In retrospect, these laws can be seen as one of the boldest social experiments in history. The result effectively abolished marriage as a legal contract. As a result, it's no longer possible to form a binding agreement to create a family.

Feminists Promoted No-Fault Divorce

Though the changes were passed largely by and for the legal business, the ideological engine that has never been properly appreciated was organized feminism. Not generally perceived as a gender battle—and never one they wished to advertise—divorce became the most devastating weapon in the arsenal of feminism, because it creates millions of gender battles on the most personal level. Germaine Greer openly celebrates divorce as the foremost indicator of feminist triumph: "Exactly the thing that people tear their hair out about is exactly the thing I am very proud of," she tells the Australian newspaper.

This is hardly new. As early as the American Revolution and throughout the 19th century, "divorce became an increasingly important measure of women's political freedom as well as an expression of feminine initiative and independence," writes Whitehead. "The association of divorce with women's freedom and prerogatives remained an enduring and important feature of American divorce."

Well before the 1970s, it was the symbiosis of law and women's rights that created the divorce revolution. The National Association of Women Lawyers (NAWL) claims credit for no-fault divorce, which it describes as "the greatest project NAWL has ever undertaken." As early as 1947, the NAWL convention approved a no-fault bill. Working through the American Bar Association, NAWL convinced the National Conference of Commissioners of Uniform State Laws (NCCUSL) to produce the Uniform Marriage and Divorce Act. "By 1977, the divorce portions had been adopted by nine states," NAWL proudly notes, and "the ideal of no-fault divorce became the guiding principle for reform of divorce laws in the majority of states." By 1985, every state had no-fault divorce.

Today, feminist operatives employ similar strategies to encourage divorce worldwide, often inserting it unnoticed and unopposed into programs for "human rights," and unilateral divorce is now one of the first measures implemented by leftist governments. When Spain's socialists came to power last year, their three domestic priorities were legalized abortion, same-sex marriage, and liberalized divorce. Iranian feminist Emadeddin Baghi writes in the *Washington Post* that "a 20 percent increase in the divorce rate is a sign that traditional marriage is changing as women gain equality." And Turkey was required to withdraw a proposal to penalize adultery to gain acceptance in the European Union, while divorce liberalization counted in their favor.

Divorce Seizes Children from Fathers

The damage done by family breakdown—especially to children—is now so well known that it hardly needs laboring. Children of divorced parents suffer far more emotional and behavioral problems than do children from intact families. They are more likely to attempt suicide and to suffer poor health. They perform more poorly in school and are more inclined to become involved with drugs, alcohol, gangs, and crime. These problems continue into adulthood, when children of divorce have more trouble forming and keeping stable relationships of their own. Through divorce, they in turn pass these traits to their own children. All this entails social costs for the rest of us, giving the public an interest in family preservation.

It might be one thing if parents were colluding to inflict this on their own children, as divorce defenders like to pretend. Even given the social consequences, a case might still be made that divorce is each couple's "private decision," as Michigan Governor Jennifer Granholm recently claimed when she vetoed a mild reform bill. But in the vast majority of cases, only one of the parents imposes divorce on the children and the other parent. Astoundingly, the parent who inflicts the divorce on the children is also the one most likely to retain custody of them. In such cases, divorce isn't remotely private; it amounts to a public seizure of the innocent spouse's children and invasion of his or her parental rights, perpetrated by our governments and using our tax dollars.

Indeed, civil freedom is perhaps the least appreciated casualty of unilateral divorce. G.K. Chesterton once warned that the family is the most enduring check on government power and that divorce and democracy were ultimately incompatible. The repressive measures being enacted against divorced fathers—most of whom never agree to a divorce and are legally faultless—now include incarcerations without trial or charge, coerced confessions, and the creation of special courts and forced labor facilities.

Politicians Afraid to Challenge No-Fault Divorce

No one should have any illusions that reversing these trends will be easy. The political interests that abolished marriage in the first place have only grown more wealthy and powerful off the system they created. Thirty-five years of unrestrained divorce have created a multibillion-dollar industry and given vast numbers of people a vested interest in it. Divorce and custody are the cash cow of the judiciary and directly employ a host of federal, state, and local officials, plus private hangers-on. More largely, the societal ills left by broken families create further employment and power for even larger armies of officials. So entrenched has divorce become within our political economy, and so diabolical is its ability to insinuate itself throughout our political culture, that even critics seem to have developed a stake in having something to bemoan. Hardly anyone has an incentive to bring it under control.

In contrast with gay marriage, abortion, and pornography, politicians studiously avoid divorce laws. "Opposing gay marriage or gays in the military is for Republicans an easy, juicy, risk-free issue," Maggie Gallagher writes. "The message [is] that at all costs we should keep divorce off the political agenda." No American politician of national stature has ever challenged involuntary divorce. "Democrats did not want to anger their large constituency among women who saw easy divorce as a hard-won freedom and prerogative," observes Whitehead. "Republicans did not want to alienate their upscale constituents or their libertarian wing, both of whom tended to favor easy divorce, nor did they want to call attention to the divorces among their own leadership." In his famous denunciation of single parenthood, Vice President Dan Quayle was careful to make clear, "I am not talking about a situation where there is a divorce." The exception proves the rule. When Pope John Paul II spoke out against divorce in January 2002, he was roundly attacked from the Right as well as the Left.

Public Concern About Broken Families

Yet politicians can no longer ignore the issue. For one thing, the logic of the same-sex marriage controversy may force us to confront divorce, since the silence is becoming conspicuous and threatens to undermine the credibility of marriage proponents. "People who won't censure divorce carry no special weight as defenders of marriage," writes columnist Froma Harrop. "Moral authority doesn't come cheap."

There is also evidence that the public is becoming not only aware of, but increasingly impatient with, fallout from

Marriage Commitment Not Legally Protected

No-fault divorce has contributed to a 25% increase in the rate of divorce all by itself, and has perversely contributed to an increase in cohabitation as adults have less and less confidence that a marriage commitment will receive significant legal protection.

Reversing the trend toward cohabitation will require a cultural awakening which reestablishes the view that personal happiness is a function of high-trust and lasting relationships.

Bryan Fischer,
"No-Fault Divorce, Cohabitation Harmful to Families,"
September 27, 2007. www.renewamerica.us.

broken families. A 1999 *NBC News/Wall Street Journal* poll found that 78 percent of Americans see the high divorce rate as a serious problem, and a *Time/CNN* poll found that 61 percent believe it should be harder for couples with young children to divorce. "Taxpayers who have preserved their own marriages through personal integrity and sacrifice," Christensen suggests, "may find it puzzling and offensive that state officials appear so willing to dissolve marriages and to collectivize the costs."

Ban on Divorce Won't Work

Thus far, most proposals aimed at addressing the divorce issue have been limited to the least costly—and least effective. Requirements that divorcing couples undergo waiting periods and counseling have passed in some states (and form the substance of most "covenant marriage" laws). But at best, such provisions merely delay the outcome. At worst, they place psychotherapists on the government payroll or force involuntary litigants to hire them. Either way, the therapists develop a stake in more divorce.

On the other hand, while simply banning groundless divorce shows more determination, it's unlikely to be very effective, since it isn't practical to force people to live together. An Arizona bill introduced in 2003, for example, stipulated that a court "shall not decree a dissolution of the marriage on grounds of incompatibility if: a) the wife is pregnant; or b) the couple has ever had a child." Such measures may discourage breakups among observant Christians and could provide some legal redress against desertion. But as Chesterton observed, a ban on divorce is mostly, in practice, a ban on remarriage. Under such a provision a spouse could simply separate (with the children) and live in permanent adultery with a new paramour.

Such schemes lend plausibility to some of the irrelevant arguments of divorce promoters: "No good can come from forcing people to remain in loveless marriages, even in the misguided belief that somehow it is better for the children," runs an editorial in the *Daily Herald* of Provo, Utah, opposing a mild reform bill recently introduced. "Is it really good for children to be raised in a home by two parents who don't love each other and who fight all the time but who are forced to stay because of the law?"

Children Oppose Divorce

These questions are red herrings. Divorce today does not necessarily indicate marital conflict and is less likely to be the last resort for a troubled marriage than a sudden power grab. Most divorces are initiated with little warning and often involve child snatchings. In 25 percent of marriage breakdowns, writes Margaret Brinig of Iowa State University, the man has "no clue" there is a problem until the woman says she wants out. A University of Exeter study found that in over half the cases there was no recollection of major conflict before the separation. "The assumption that parental conflict will cease at divorce is not only invalid," writes Patricia Morgan; "divorce itself instigates conflict which continues into the post-divorce period."

Further, as Judith Wallerstein and Sandra Blakeslee found, few children are pleased with divorce, even when severe conflict exists. "Children can be quite content even when their parents' marriage is profoundly unhappy for one or both partners," they write. "Only one in ten children in our study experienced relief when their parents divorced. These were mostly older children in families where there had been open violence." Divorce and separation almost always have a more detrimental effect on children than even high-conflict marriages. "The misery their parents may feel in an unhappy marriage is usually less significant than the changes [the children] have to go through after a divorce," says Neil Kalter, a University of Michigan psychologist. Surveys of children by Ann Mitchell and J.T. Landis found that most recalled a happy family life before the breakup.

Fault Should Be Required for Divorce

In any case, limiting no-fault divorce will never force people to live together—though done properly, it will provide strong incentives to work at their marriages rather than dissolve them. Reforming divorce laws, first of all, means re-introducing fault for violating the marital contract. It will, in effect, restore justice to the legal proceedings. "The alternative to liberal or 'no-fault' divorce is not no divorce," writes Whelan, "but divorce which is granted only after due legal process to establish fault." The obvious counterargument, that failed marriages often entail imperfections on both sides, does not justify abandoning all standards of justice. "There is fault on both sides in every human relationship," Fred Hanson acknowledged when the laws were enacted. "The faults, however, are far from equal.

No secular society can be operated on the theory that all faults are equal." Hanson was the dissenting member of NCCUSL, which designed no-fault laws. "To do justice between parties without regard to fault is an impossibility," he warned. "I wonder what's to become of the maxim that no man shall profit by his own wrong—or woman either, for that matter."

Tragically, we now have the answer in today's perversion of the criminal justice system by divorce-related accusations of domestic "abuse." Patently fabricated charges are now rampant in divorce courts, mostly to secure child custody and remove fathers, and the cry of "trapping women in abusive marriages" has become the principal argument against fault-based divorce. The irony is telling, since physical violence obviously is and always has been grounds for divorce. The argument also reveals the totalitarian nature of today's feminism. What feminists object to is being held to the same standards of evidence as everyone else by having to prove their accusations. Fault divorce would entail the "burden of proving that abuse had occurred," argues the *Daily Herald*. "It's not easy to accumulate medical records detailing injuries, eyewitnesses, and a police record of domestic violence calls to the house." It isn't? But that's precisely what the rest of us must do when we accuse others of vicious crimes. What feminists want—and already have—is the power to trample the presumption of innocence and due process of law in order to evict fathers on accusations of ill-defined "abuse" that cannot be proven because, in many cases, it did not take place at all.

Protect the Innocent Spouse

This is the inevitable consequence of abolishing objective standards and allowing judges to create infractions out of whatever subjective grievance or "abuse" a tearful spouse invokes. To operate effectively, fault must entail objective, enumerated, and proven grounds that are understood at the time of marriage. These grounds may vary somewhat among jurisdictions, but spouses must have a reasonably predictable expectation of the consequences of specific misbehaviors and violations of the marital contract. This basic principle of justice is required of all other laws in a free society.

Further, to effectively deter divorce, fault must entail substantial consequences. Or stated more positively, innocence must carry substantial protections. While property considerations are not trivial, most important is that marriage must protect an innocent spouse's right to be left in peace with his or her children. Feminists complain that this punishes women for leaving a bad marriage. But strictly speaking (and aside from the question of whose behavior made it a bad marriage), it need entail no punishment at all. It simply allows an innocent spouse to invoke the protections for which he or she originally married.

VIEWPOINT 2

> *"If two people don't want to be married, why try the case?"*

Requiring Fault for Divorce Is Harmful

Nahal Toosi

Nahal Toosi argues in the following viewpoint that the requirement of fault to justify divorce is outdated and harmful. To get divorced quickly, she says, parties sometimes must lie, move, or tarnish their own reputations. Requiring fault for divorce, she asserts, wastes valuable judicial time. Toosi contends that the fault requirement sometimes is used as a bargaining chip in division of property. Fault requirements draw attention away from the real issues—dividing up marital property, she says. Toosi writes for the Associated Press.

As you read, consider the following questions:

1. What is the only state that won't allow speedy divorce without proof of fault, according to the author?
2. One type of fault that can be grounds for divorce, according to the author, is "constructive abandonment." What does that term mean?

Nahal Toosi, "Unhappy Matrimony: NY Divorce Law," SFGate.com, March 29, 2007.

3. In an example the author cites in the article, why did it take more than a day to pick a jury for a divorce case?

Chana and Simon Taub can't stand each other.

He claims she is a gold-digging liar. She claims he abused her. Things got so nasty during their divorce case that a court-ordered wall was put up in the feuding spouses' Brooklyn house to keep them apart.

It would seem like an open-and-shut divorce case, with no shortage of reasons to justify ending the marriage once and for all. But it is never that easy in New York, where you can get just about anything except a fast, blameless divorce.

New York is the only state that won't allow the speedy dissolution of a marriage without proof that one spouse is somehow at fault, experts say. Adultery is sufficient grounds, but irreconcilable differences are not. "He beats me" (with proof) works, but "We grew apart" doesn't cut it.

Outdated System Promotes Lying

The system has been ridiculed as hopelessly outdated, and sometimes results in endless litigation and spouses leaving the state to evade the law. This week, in what some see as more proof of the law's absurdity, a jury denied the bickering Taubs a divorce.

"I think it's an anachronistic, completely inefficient process," said Bernard Clair, a divorce lawyer. "Today, divorce is really about dividing an economic partnership. The dirty laundry aspects play no role except to jazz up the clients and distract them from the real issues of the case."

Under New York divorce law, couples can split up without either spouse being assigned blame, but only if they first sign a division-of-property agreement and live apart for a year. Couples who want to end a marriage more quickly than that have been known to lie, move or tarnish their own reputations.

Fault Divorce Can Cause Expense, Delay, and Trauma

Proponents of no-fault divorce certainly believe it is more than an empty device. The New York State Matrimonial Commission of 2006, which recommended that the state adopt no-fault divorce, found "substantial evidence [showing that] fault allegations and fault trials add significantly to the cost, delay, and trauma of matrimonial litigation and are, in many cases, used by litigants to achieve a tactical advantage."

Heidi Bruggink, "Detoxifying Divorce," Judicial Reports, *November 11, 2007.*

If the desire for a divorce is mutual, but neither side wants to wait a year, one common ruse is to have one party take the blame. A popular ground is "constructive abandonment," in which one spouse alleges the other won't have sex. The other spouse agrees not to contest the allegation.

Another approach is what Clair calls "watered-down cruel and inhuman treatment."

The plaintiff, (the wife, let's say) can claim, "He told me he didn't love me anymore, that he wanted his freedom, that he had made a mistake from the beginning." The husband neither admits nor denies the charge.

The moving option often comes into play when the desire to divorce is not mutual. But it doesn't always work.

During his nearly decade-long attempt to get a divorce, Charles Rudick moved to Vermont for 18 months. But his divorce there was denied after the state determined he wasn't really committed to living in Vermont.

Rudick, now 64, said he wanted out of his marriage because he and his wife had grown apart and he was in love with another woman. Eventually, the two came to terms. The divorce was granted on the grounds that he abandoned her.

"It's just ridiculous that we're so backward and antiquated in this state," said Rudick, a retired environmental engineer from Clifton Park.

Fault Used as a Bargaining Chip

No-fault divorce laws became popular beginning in the 1960s, but efforts to introduce such a system in New York have long failed. The main reason, observers say, is the lobbying strength of the Roman Catholic Church and the state chapter of the National Organization for Women.

To Catholic leaders, marriage is a sacred contract that should not be ended on a whim. The women's organization views a no-fault system as biased against women.

"The moneyed spouse, with no-fault, can literally hide the assets, take off, get married before the wife even knows what hit her," said Marcia Pappas, head of the state chapter of NOW.

A fault system gives the woman a bargaining chip, Pappas said. For example, she can deny her husband a divorce until she is happy with her share of the property.

Men can use that bargaining chip, too. In the case of the Taubs, the couple separated by the wall, former sweater manufacturer Simon Taub has contested his wife's divorce action, partly because he denies her claim of abuse, and partly because he wants to agree on a division of property first. Chana Taub went the "cruel and inhuman treatment" route as grounds for divorce.

Wasting the Court's Time

The Taub case has dragged on for about two years. The issue of whether a divorce could be granted finally went before a jury, which rejected the cruel-and-inhuman-treatment claim and denied Chana Taub a divorce Wednesday.

Neither spouse is sure what to do next, their attorneys said.

"A lot of judicial time is wasted," said Chana Taub's lawyer, Irvin Rosenthal. "If two people don't want to be married, why try the case?"

Simon Taub's lawyer, Abe Konstam, agreed and complained that it took more than a day to pick a jury because so many candidates said they wouldn't want to apply the state's fault requirement.

The New York City bar supports a no-fault divorce law, as does the state's chief judge, and the state Women's Bar Association backed the idea in 2004 after long opposing it. But there is no sign the law is about to be changed.

VIEWPOINT 3

> *"Staying with both parents is in the child's best interest if it's not dangerous, either physically or emotionally for the child."*

Joint Physical Custody Is Best for Children

Marilyn Gardner

In the following viewpoint, Marilyn Gardner argues that joint physical custody is in the best interests of children with divorced parents. More families are choosing joint physical custody, because fathers have become increasingly important in childrearing and they have found the role of the father to be essential in children's development. Gardner argues that joint physical custody can also be best for the parents because it encourages communication. The author emphasizes that it is essential for the parents to work together to devise a shared parenting plan that allows the child to have a home with both parents. Marilyn Gardner is a staff writer at The Christian Science Monitor.

1. Daniel Hogan, executive director of Fathers & Families, estimates that joint physical custody is awarded what percent of the time?

Marilyn Gardner, "Yours, Mine, Then Yours Again," *Christian Science Monitor*, May 3, 2006. Reproduced by permission from *Christian Science Monitor*, (www.csmonitor.com).

2. What are some cases in which joint physical custody could not work, according to the viewpoint?
3. What is "parallel parenting," and why does the author caution against it?

Ever since his parents separated nearly two years ago and then divorced, Danny Hechter has become a master of logistics, dividing his time equally between two homes in suburban Minneapolis. Sunday through Tuesday, the seventh-grader lives with his mother, Lynn Sadoff. From after school on Wednesday until Saturday morning, he stays with his father, Rich Hechter. Saturday noon the three meet for Danny's bowling league. Saturday afternoon and evening are flexible.

"We decided on an exact 50-50 split," says Ms. Sadoff, a hospital publicist. "He had very strong relationships with both of us."

Their arrangement makes them part of a growing band of divorced parents trying to create more equitable arrangements to care for their children. Instead of the traditional approach, in which children live full time with one parent—usually the mother—and spend weekends and some holidays with the other parent, these families split their time. Some choose a 30/70 division, while others prefer a 40/60 or 50/50 sharing.

More Families Are Choosing Joint Physical Custody Arrangements

"More and more men are doing more child rearing during the marriage," says Sharyn Sooho, cofounder of Divorcenet.com "As a result, more men are seeking significant parenting roles after divorce, sometimes asking to be primary residential parents."

No national statistics track the number of parents with shared-parenting arrangements. But Daniel Hogan, executive director of Fathers & Families, an advocacy group in Boston, estimates that joint physical custody is awarded 10 to 30 percent of the time, depending on the state.

"It's increasing," he says.

Eleven states have laws that include some presumption of joint physical custody, Mr. Hogan adds. "Only five states say expressly that it's fine to award joint custody even if one party disagrees. It's always at the discretion of the judge to decide if it's in the best interest of the children."

Even those who generally support shared parenting offer a caveat: Staying with both parents is in the child's best interest "only if it's not dangerous, either physically or emotionally for the child," says Mr. Hechter, a family law attorney.

He finds that shared parenting works best when parents reside in close proximity and in the same school district. He and Sadoff live just eight blocks apart, making it easy for Danny to go back and forth.

Successful arrangements also depend on parents' work schedules, their child-rearing skills, and the ages of the children. "The youngest children need one main home base," says Wendy Allen, a psychotherapist in Santa Barbara, Calif., who works with custody issues.

Some critics argue that many children of all ages need one primary home. Lots of shuttling back and forth can be tough, they say. Supporters counter that having a close relationship with both parents outweighs the disadvantage of two homes.

Good for Parents Too

Some divorced parents actually find that the need to maintain regular contact with each other has helped them to forge a good relationship.

"We've been able to look beyond all the ill will and negative feelings that come up," Hechter says. "Both parents have to put their bitterness behind."

That can be a challenge. "If it's an every-other-weekend thing, you're less involved," says Shari, a mother of two on Long Island who asked to be identified only by her first name to protect her sons' privacy. "If they're going to their dad's

Study Finds Joint Custody Better

The most comprehensive assessment of the effects of joint custodial arrangements was a meta-analysis conducted in 2002 that reviewed thirty-three studies that focused on the adjustment of children in sole and joint (physical or legal) arrangements. Bauserman examined the relationship between any joint (physical or legal) arrangement and a number of child-outcome measures, including general adjustment, behavioral and emotional adjustments, family relations, academic performance, and adjustment to living in a divorced family. When possible, he also controlled for parental conflict. He found that across the board, children from joint-custody homes had better outcomes than children in sole-custody homes, with an effect size that he described as "slightly greater than what would be considered a small effect size." He also broke down the analyses by custody type and found, regardless of whether the study focused on legal custody or physical custody, that children in joint arrangements fared better than children in sole custodial arrangements.

Emily M. Douglas, Mending Broken Families: Social Policies for Divorced Families: How Effective Are They? *Lanham, MD: Rowman & Littlefield Publishers, Inc., 2006.*

house this evening, I have to be in touch with him. It's not easy, when the person you're dealing with is the person you made this enormous break with. It's definitely harder, but for the children's sake I think it's better that they have both parents in their lives."

Her teen sons spend 30 percent of the time with their father and 70 percent with her. Calling her former spouse "a good dad and a good ex-husband," she adds, "Considering the circumstances, this was and is a good solution for the children."

Like many offspring who shuttle between two homes, Shari's boys have two sets of certain possessions, as does Sadoff's son, Danny. "We try to have what he needs at both homes—two computers, two sets of research materials," Sadoff says.

"The child must be very well organized, or Mom and Dad must be willing to communicate well and cart stuff back and forth," says Lisa Cohn of Portland, Ore., who was divorced 14 years ago and has remarried. One recent weekend her 17-year-old son, Travis, realized that his soccer gear was at his father's. "His dad met us at the game with his uniform," Ms. Cohn says.

For them, such meetings are amicable. "Over the years, my ex and I have learned to get along very well," Cohn says. The two sit together at school activities and meet with Travis's teachers together. Last month, when Travis went to his first prom, he dressed at his father's house, then went to his mom's so she could see his first tux.

Not all parents can manage such connections. Isolina Ricci, author of "Mom's House, Dad's House for Kids," refutes a common misperception that shared parenting helps to guarantee that the children will be all right. "It doesn't work that way," she says. "Sometimes it is a very conflicted arrangement. That conflict is not a plus for the children."

Importance of Communication

Dr. Ricci cautions against what she calls parallel parenting. The parents share child rearing, but she likens them to two separate countries. They do not talk to each other and may not have any conversation about the children. Parents with dissimilar lifestyles can leave children equally confused. At one house, they might stay up until 11 p.m. or later with unlimited TV watching and no homework, Ricci says. The other house might be much more structured, with bedtime at 9 o'clock and limited TV.

"When parents have different lifestyles, when they are unwilling to compromise . . . so rules are more consistent, it can be very stressful for children," Ricci says. "It's hard to shift gears."

Although Ricci calls herself a "big supporter" of shared parenting, she cautions that it should not be a catchall for difficult situations. "You can have an old-fashioned parenting arrangement that works just fine."

Ricci sees a push on some fronts for shared parenting to be the norm. But she emphasizes that parents have an obligation "to take very seriously what it's going to take to be an effective parent. It requires more sophistication, more skill."

Some parents who cannot communicate well in person keep in touch by e-mail. Others coordinate children's schedules on special websites.

Even if parents' relationships are strained, Ms. Sooho urges them to make every effort to be pleasant during pickups and dropoffs. "If the parents are reasonably calm during the transitions, if they are mature and gracious, and say 'Hello, how are you?' [to the other parent], children are usually fine with it."

Mr. Hogan expects that in the short run, passing legislation on shared parenting could be "very tough." As fathers'-rights groups become better organized and more vocal, he says, opponents are also gaining strength. But in the long term, he thinks supporters "will gradually be able to convince the legislatures that shared parenting is a good idea."

Last Thursday evening, nearly 200 members of Fathers & Families turned out in Boston for a meeting on the issue. "Without the law behind you, you don't really have shared parenting," said Michael Paolino of Hampton, N.H., a participant.

Shifting Attitudes

As attitudes toward postdivorce child rearing change, so does the vocabulary. Instead of "visitation schedule," some divorce lawyers and judges now say "parenting schedule," Sooho says. Rather than "custodial and noncustodial parents," they refer to the "primary residential parent" and the "nonresidential parent."

"The words 'custody' and 'visitation' belong to prisons and hospitals," Ricci says. "This may be useful language for the legal system, but not for families."

By whatever name, these complex arrangements produce varied opinions. Neil Gussman of Philadelphia, who was divorced 10 years ago and is remarried, has two teenage daughters who take a positive view. They leave for school from one parent's house and go home to the other.

"I have asked several times over the years if the girls would like a different arrangement, but so far, seeing both parents nearly every day is very important to them," he says.

Shari is cautious: "My sons do get tired of having two of everything," she says. "I don't think we're really going to know how they perceive it until the storms of adolescence pass. But they see, on a regular basis, how their parents put forth the effort to continue this over what is now a very long time."

Looking back over the past eight years, she adds, "It's been an interesting ride. You have to be really committed to it and be willing to do the work to make it happen. But I think it's worth it."

VIEWPOINT 4

> "Kids are saying that what they really like is one solid base to call home."

Joint Physical Custody Creates Problems for Children

Eleanor Bailey

Eleanor Bailey argues in the following viewpoint that joint custody can be harmful to children. Requiring children to move from home to home creates constant upheaval, she says. Divorced parents, she argues, often have different parenting styles, creating confusion and anxiety. She asserts that joint custody often is a decision chosen by the parents without considering the best interests of the children. The author contends that research shows that children prefer to have one home. Bailey writes for The Mail on Sunday.

As you read, consider the following questions:

1. According to a study cited by the author, joint custody often is chosen not for the best interests of the child but instead for what reason?
2. Why, according to experts cited by the author, are both parents not equally important to children?

Eleanor Bailey, "Are You Playing Pass the Parcel with Your Child?" *The Mail on Sunday*, December 10, 2006. Reproduced by permission.

3. Why do divorced parents have difficulty cooperating in shared custody arrangements, in the view of the author?

It might be the perfect family holiday for a 20-year-old—a weekend in East Hampton on the beach with rock star dad and friends, followed by lunch in a fashionable restaurant with a mother who's flown in especially from 3,000 miles away—but for two-year-old Beatrice McCartney it was all too much. According to startled residents of the exclusive seaside resort, the normally placid little girl had to be removed screaming and sobbing from lunch with Mummy and bundled into a waiting car by the minder. The golden-haired toddler was 'very distressed and confused', said someone eating in the restaurant at the time.

And she was probably equally distressed by the distance between her parents at her recent third birthday party. Although both of them attended, they exchanged barely a word as hostilities have reached such a peak that they can hardly stand being in the same room as each other.

Ex-Beatle Sir Paul [McCartney] is as hands-on a parent as multimillionaires get—hanging out in the nursery playground where lesser celebrities would send the nanny—and he is widely expected to apply for custody of his daughter. Since Heather [Mills] is unlikely to give Beatrice up, the little girl's routine is likely to remain chaotic.

Joint Custody Traumatizes Children

It's because both parents want her so much that Beatrice is turning into that modern phenomenon—what you might call a pass-the-parcel child: handed between parents, between time zones, spending one week in one continent, the next in another, in different homes and among different people, often strangers.

This might seem the only way to fit a child into the complicated lifestyles of highflying parents, but it can leave children confused, traumatised, and unable to cope with the constant upheaval. For, just as the government has announced that judges should allow children from as young as primary age to speak up in court about which parent they want to live with and how much contact they want to have, so a piece of research has been published in which kids are saying that what they really like is one solid base to call home.

Parent Problems, published by the Economic and Social Research Council, tracked 60 children through their parents' divorces and the years afterwards.

It found that where shared custody was arranged it was often to support 'over-needy parents' rather than because it is the best arrangement for the child.

Having Two Homes Confuses Children

'Having two homes is like putting your life in a couple of carrier bags every two weeks,' said one child in the research. Another said she had to swap houses every two days, but felt 'under pressure not to say anything' about changing the situation for fear of upsetting her mum and dad. 'If you're constantly moving you feel a bit lonely,' said a 14-year-old. 'I was getting mixed up about who I was,' complained another.

'Any arrangement can work,' stresses the co-author of the report, Dr. Bren Neale, senior research fellow at the Centre for Research on Family, Kinship and Childhood at the University of Leeds, 'but it needs to be managed with flexibility.

Splitting childcare 50:50 in the name of "fairness" can become a tyranny to live under.' Scottish psychologist Dr. Jack Boyle is more adamant.

'To parents who think it's a good idea to share parenting, I say, "OK then, let the child stay in the house and you two swap houses every week."

'They don't want to go backwards and forwards; they have their own lives.'

Both Parents Aren't Equally Important

And it's no argument to say that both parents are equally important to the child, because they aren't. There is always one main caregiver, usually the mother.' This last, perhaps rather unfashionable, point hit home to Siobhan, 35-year-old mother of Toby, five, and Isobel, three, only in hindsight, when it became clear that her children found it hard to cope with their pass-the-parcel arrangements.

'My ex and I arranged to share the kids 50:50 one week with me, one week with him through a mediation service, because we both wanted custody but didn't want the trauma of going to court. It seemed like a sensible, modern solution—John is a great, emotionally involved father and having the children live with him half the time was a way of continuing that. But the bottom line was that I had been their main emotional support, and they found being without me for a week at a time very difficult.

Different Parenting Styles Confuse Children

'Every time it came to the end of my week and I had to drive the children over to John's new flat, they would both be clingy and crying. They found all the chopping and changing distressing and they didn't take to his new girlfriend. She tried her best but she was unfamiliar. And John's parenting style was so different that it confused them all the more. He would keep them up with his friends in the evenings—they were always meeting new people and he let them eat whatever they liked.

'I felt they thrived best on routine and insisted they lived by my rules when with me. It's all very well having their dad do things differently if it's once a month, as a treat, but living two completely opposite lifestyles tore the children in half.

'Isobel was only 18 months—too young to be shunted about—and Toby suffered because Isobel grabbed more attention. He tried so hard to be the strong big brother, it was

Potential Disadvantages of Joint Custody

Even if joint custody has advantages for parents and children, there are costs to this arrangement. For one thing, joint custody poses problems for a parent who wants to move to a different area. For another, even if parents stay in the same area, joint custody leads to less stability for children, who must be shuttled between their parents, encountering differences in household rules, parental expectations, and sometimes even socioeconomic status as they move from one household to the other. Children who moved more frequently between their parents were at risk for emotional and behavioral problems in one study of high-conflict parents, probably because frequent access created more opportunities for disagreements between the parents.

Most critically, joint custody ties parents together—even if they hate each other. Joint custody is a painful yoke when parents are in conflict or didn't want joint custody in the first place. . . . Because joint custody typically fosters more contact between parents, these arrangements can maintain highly dysfunctional parental relationships. Children who feel caught in the middle when their parents fight face particularly negative outcomes. If both parents have an equal say in any decision making pertaining to their children, disagreements and open conflict between parents can set off confusion, loyalty conflicts, and maladjustment in children. Any benefits derived from frequent access to both parents are diminished by the strain of continued exposure to parents' conflict.

Alison Clarke-Stewart and Cornelia Brentano, Divorce: Causes and Consequences. *New Haven: Yale University Press, 2006.*

heartbreaking. I would drop him off and watch his lip wobbling as he waved goodbye from the porch—a three-year-old shouldn't be under that kind of pressure. It began to seem cruel.

Parental Cooperation Difficult for Divorced Parents

'We thought we were putting the kids first, but we weren't: it was all about us getting our fair turn. It did strike me as ironic that this wouldn't have been a problem in the bad old days when a typical dad was a remote, emotionally distant figure who was often never heard from again after a divorce. Looking back, our 50:50 arrangements were unworkable, because we couldn't give each other an inch and we were fighting too hard to think straight.' It is this, says Jane Robey, chief executive of the Family Mediation service, which makes shared parenting so difficult. Living a complicated pass-the-parcel life can only work for a child if both parents are cooperating and making the process smooth and simple—and this is unlikely when a couple is in the throes of breaking up. 'People in the midst of divorce are typically very emotional, angry and guilty,' she says. 'It can take two years to restabilise. Once the sexual relationship dies so does all the trust.

'For example, if another mother had taken your child out for the afternoon and rang to say she was going to be late coming back, you wouldn't think twice about it, but if it's your former spouse, you immediately see it as a terrible thing, unfit parenting, neglect.' Ideally, feuding parents need to reinvent themselves as professional partners in the business of bringing up the children. Not easy, but, Dr. Neale says, in tune with the government's insistence that children need a say in their post-divorce lives: that shared parenting works best when adults treat their children as citizens within the family, with rights and boundaries that everybody understands and where parents consult their children as much as possible.

'Children need to feel they have their own space and not that their time is allocated to one parent or another in a restricting way,' says Dr. Neale.

Joint Custody Can Cause Anxiety

Siobhan's shared parenting experiment lasted just over a year, until Toby's first school parents' evening, which both parents attended, but as separate agents.

'There we got the wakeup call. Toby's teacher said she was concerned that he was suffering from anxiety and found concentration difficult. By then we had enough distance to be able to talk more sensibly. We agreed that, instead of the 50:50 routine, the kids would live with me and visit John at weekends.

'Luckily John accepted that he didn't need to have half of their time to be a full parent. I'm more cooperative, too, now that I don't feel I'm competing for my own children. It's not perfect but it's better. . . .'

'People still don't fully appreciate the impact divorce has on kids,' says Relate therapist Paula Hall, who is writing a book on divorce. 'They block out their individual responsibility.' And where that responsibility might once have been all about staying in touch with the children, now perhaps it means there are times when, for the sake of those children, one parent has to let go a little.

Signs That Joint Custody Isn't Working

Is co-parenting working for your child? To find out, you should watch them closely, says Relate's Paula Hall:

- Look out for adverse reactions such as your child becoming more withdrawn or aggressive, or regressing into younger behaviour such as bed wetting.

- Watch out for the child who buries unhappiness under complete compliance with the new arrangements.
- Monitor your child closely. Ask him or her frequently, but casually, 'How do you think things are going?'
- Talk to their teachers to check they aren't showing any signs of anxiety at school.
- Give yourself a reality check: how much of your parenting choices are influenced by anger? Can you acknowledge your ex-partner's value as a parent?

Periodical Bibliography

The following articles have been selected to supplement the diverse views presented in this chapter.

Michelle Adams and Scott Coltrane	"Framing Divorce Reform: Media, Morality, and the Politics of Family," *Family Process*, March 1, 2007.
Douglas W. Allen, Krishna Pendakur, and Wing Suen	"No-Fault Divorce and the Compression of Marriage Ages," *Economic Inquiry*, July 1, 2006.
James Bogle	"Do the Courts Regard Fathers as Redundant?" *National Observer—Australia and World Affairs*, June 22, 2005.
Amy M. Donley and James D. Wright	"For Richer or For Poorer: The Impact of State-Level Legislation on Marriage, Divorce, and Other Outcomes," *Sociological Spectrum*, vol. 28, no. 2, March-April 2008.
Kristie M. Engemann and Michael T. Owyang	"Splittsville: The Economics of Unilateral Divorce," *Regional Economist*, January 1, 2008.
Mark Feinberg, Marni L. Kan, and E. Mavis Hetherington	"The Longitudinal Influence of Coparenting Conflict on Parental Negativity and Adolescent Maladjustment," *Journal of Marriage & Family*, vol. 69, no. 3, August 2007.
Christopher Hudson	"The Wife Who Changed History," *Daily Mail*, January 18, 2008.
Anne Kingston	"Upstairs, Mom; Downstairs, Dad," *Maclean's*, vol. 120, no. 42, October 29, 2007.
James Andrew Miller	"Preparing for a Broken Home," *New York Times*, vol. 156, no. 54007, July 16, 2007.
Michelle Mitcham-Smith and Wilma J. Henry	"High-Conflict Divorce Solutions: Parenting Coordination as an Innovative Co-Parenting Intervention," *Family Journal*, October 2007.
Cheryl Wetzstein	"No-Fault Law Tied to Rise in Divorces," *The Washington Times* (DC), July 17, 2007.

Chapter 4

Can the Negative Effects Of Divorce Be Minimized?

Chapter Preface

Studies show that divorce is one of the most stressful life events a person will experience, second only to the death of a spouse. Yet divorce is something a substantial number of Americans will experience. How can the negative effects of divorce be minimized?

Most experts say minimizing conflict is the key. As psychotherapist Samuel M. Portnoy has observed, divorce inflicts deep wounds. It is easy to criticize divorcing couples who lash out and fight with their soon-to-be exes, but as conflict management expert and mediator Daniel Bjerkness has pointed out, "The experience of conflict [of divorce] causes them to be at their worst." Divorce attorney Robyn Lynne Ryan has observed that when faced with an unwanted divorce, a temptation exists to react in extreme ways. She recommends that what a divorcing party needs to do, however, is "rise above it all."

Children can be innocent victims of the divorce conflict. To protect the children, Portnoy recommends a divorcing party to "above all avoid conflict with your ex-spouse." Portnoy says that "[i]t would not be unreasonable to sum up the findings of childhood adjustment to parental divorce in one conclusion: if the parents can maintain a civil and mutually supportive relationship the kids will do better."

Divorcing couples with children necessarily have a relationship that lasts beyond the divorce. Bjerkness reports that "[m]any researchers have found that it is not the divorce itself that causes children's problems, but rather it is the quality of the relationship and parenting by custodial and noncustodial parents after the divorce that has the greatest impact."

How can divorcing parties minimize conflict and maximize civility? Many recommend avoiding litigation—litigation has winners and losers, escalates tension, and can prevent parents from working cooperatively for the best interests of the child. A messy divorce also can create grudges that provide fuel for ongoing hostility after the divorce.

Mediation is an alternative to litigation. Dr. Robert E. Emery conducted a twelve-year study of mediation in divorce, using a sample of divorce cases in which families had filed for contested custody hearings. Families were randomly assigned to mediation (average length five hours) or to remain in the adversary system. Of those who went to mediation, less than 20 percent ended up before a family court judge, as compared with 75 percent of those who remained in the adversary system. Furthermore, the long-term effect of mediation on the relationship between the children and the noncustodial parent was marked. Where mediation occurred, twelve years after the divorce 54 percent of the noncustodial parents spoke with their child at least weekly, compared to 14 percent who used litigation and the national average of 18 percent.

Collaborative divorce is another alternative to litigation. While similar to mediation, collaborative divorce also employs psychologists and financial experts. Proponents claim that these additional resources make collaborative divorce superior. Opponents claim collaborative divorce is unnecessary in most cases, can create ethical problems for the attorney, and can result in additional expense and delay.

Though divorce begins as a stressful event, some argue that it can be a cloud with a silver lining. Karen Ely, author of *Daring to Dream: Reflections on the Year I Found Myself*, and Mel Kantzler, author of *Divorce: A New Opportunity for Personal Growth*, suggest that divorce can lead to rebirth and a fresh start for the next stage of life.

VIEWPOINT 1

> *"Collaborative divorce offers constructive, comprehensive, multidisciplinary professional support that responds to the actual complexities of divorce as people experience it."*

Collaborative Divorce Works

Pauline Tesler and Peggy Thompson

Pauline Tesler and Peggy Thompson argue in the following viewpoint that collaborative divorce is the most effective way to address the issues that really matter to divorcing parties. Collaborative divorce, they assert, avoids litigation and provides support that is more comprehensive by using not only attorneys, but also psychologists and financial advisors. Collaborative divorce is better than mediation, they say, because it provides more resources than a mediator can provide. Tesler, an attorney, and Thompson, a psychologist, are authors of Collaborative Divorce: The Revolutionary New Way to Restructure Your Family, Resolve Legal Issues, and Move on with Your Life.

As you read, consider the following questions:

1. According to the authors, how does collaborative divorce build in protections for children?

Pauline Tesler and Peggy Thompson, *Collaborative Divorce: The Revolutionary New Way to Restructure Your Family, Resolve Legal Issues, and Move on With Your Life*. New York: HarperCollins, 2006.

2. Why, according to the authors, do old-style divorce proceedings deem many common concerns that are important to divorcing parties irrelevant?
3. When comparing mediation to collaborative divorce, what analogy do the authors use to illustrate the difference?

We know from long experience that only collaborative divorce—not old-style adversarial legal representation, and not a single mediator working with or without lawyers in the picture—views divorce as a complex experience requiring advice and counsel from multiple perspectives if it is to be navigated well. Collaborative divorce prepares you to deal with the emotional challenges and changes associated with divorce and provides the resources that can best help you make a healthy transition from married to single.

Advantages of Collaborative Divorce

Collaborative divorce builds in important protections for children, too. It informs you fully about how your children are experiencing the divorce and what they need to weather the big changes in their family structure without harm. It helps protect your future relationship with your spouse by informing both of you fully—together, at the same time—about the financial realities of your marriage and divorce in a way that eliminates pointless arguments about economic issues. It also teaches you and your spouse new ways of problem solving and conflict resolution so that you develop useful skills for addressing your differences more constructively in the future. Further, collaborative divorce

- Helps you clarify your individual and shared values and priorities
- Helps you and your spouse reach maximum consensus

- Includes complete advice about the law without using legal rights as the sole template for negotiation and resolution
- Helps you and your spouse resolve serious differences creatively and without destructive conflict
- Helps parents improve their ability to coparent after divorce
- Builds in agreements about resolution of future differences after the divorce is over
- Focuses not only on resolving past differences but also on planning for healthy responses to current challenges and on laying a strong foundation for the future after the divorce is over
- Aims toward deep resolution, not shallow peace

Disadvantages of Old-Style Divorce

We're confident that, like the people we work with every day, you want to protect yourself and your loved ones from the havoc that an old-style divorce can wreak in your lives. Let's summarize the facts you now know about old-style divorce:

- It is based on the centuries-old belief that divorce is wrong and abnormal
- It seeks to find fault and mete out punishment
- It focuses on the past
- It is premised on conflict
- It is constrained by an arbitrary legal framework intended to resolve matters of right and wrong by the exchange of money
- It aims at a deal, not deep resolution

- It fails to take into account current understandings of how people are wired, what they need in times of change, what children need during and after divorce, and how families change and restructure

What's more, we know that old-style divorce is bad for individuals, families, and communities because

- It's expensive
- It's hurtful and damaging
- It's "one size fits all"
- It deems irrelevant many common concerns that are extremely important to most people because judges can't issue enforceable orders about them
- It focuses on the past
- It encourages unrealistic expectations on the part of both spouses about what should happen in the divorce
- It resolves disputes through competing predictions of what a judge would do rather than focusing on what you and your partner can agree on
- It won't provide essential help to you or those you care about
- The emotional and social costs are incalculable

Collaborative Divorce Better Option

Luckily, we live in an era when there is finally a better option—one that can end a marriage without destroying a family or setting into motion negative effects that can bedevil family members for a lifetime.

The reasons why collaborative divorce does such a good job of helping most people achieve their own "best divorce" are simple. Collaborative divorce addresses the financial and legal matters that must be resolved in any divorce, but it does

Eliminating the Threat of Litigation

In collaborative law, the traditional approach of bargaining from a specific position, backed by threats of litigation and court intervention, is replaced by an approach that settles cases respectfully. The approach meets the needs of both parties and the children, and still involves legal counsel, but eliminates the threat or fear of court intervention at any stage.

Ronald L. Hendrix,
"The Collaborative Approach—Does It Work for Divorcing Spouses?"
DivorceNet, *March 6, 2006. www.divorcenet.com.*

so more effectively because it provides the built-in help of three professions, not just one. The design of collaborative divorce—with its team of professionals, its systematic attention to values, its emphasis on healthy relationships, and its focus on the future—takes into account the broad spectrum of what really matters to most people when their marriages end. It considers not only the two spouses but those around them who also matter to the divorcing couple and who will be both directly and indirectly affected by a good or a bad divorce: children, families, and even extended families, friends, and colleagues. It applies what we know about marriage and divorce from the realms of psychology, sociology, history, law, communication theory, conflict resolution theory, finance, and other realms in a very practical, useful, and concrete way.

Collaborative Divorce Addresses the Realities of Divorce

Unlike any other divorce conflict resolution process that has come before, collaborative divorce teams make constant use of vital information about how people are "wired," how we think, how our emotions affect our ability to communicate effectively and to process information, how we experience pain and loss, how we recover from the end of a marriage, what our children are experiencing and what they need in the divorce, and what the needs of each member of the family after the divorce are likely to be. In this way, collaborative divorce offers constructive, comprehensive, multidisciplinary professional support that responds to the actual complexities of divorce as people experience it, rather than imposing an old-fashioned, limited institutional legal point of view as the sole perspective on a complex human experience.

Collaborative Divorce Better than Mediation

When you first hear about collaborative divorce, you may think, "That's just like mediation." While it is a cousin of mediation, and while individual mediators often accomplish very good work with their clients, the mediation process itself compared to collaborative divorce is like checkers compared to 3-D chess. Through their very structure, collaborative divorce teams can consistently offer couples and families far more resources and far more powerful support for deep conflict resolution than any single mediator possibly can.

Viewpoint 

> *"Anything that you can do inside the collaborative model you can do outside the collaborative model, but the reverse isn't true."*

Collaborative Divorce Is Not Good For Most Cases

Caryn Tamber

Caryn Tamber argues in the following viewpoint that collaborative divorce is not best for most divorces. Good divorce attorneys, she argues, can settle divorce cases without resorting to collaborative divorce. She asserts that many attorneys say it is naïve to believe that the parties will voluntarily disclose all information relevant to the divorce as required in collaborative divorce. Collaborative divorce also raises ethical issues, she argues, as attorneys in collaborative divorce are obligated to disclose the other attorney's mistakes. Tamber writes for The Daily Record.

As you read, consider the following questions:

1. According to the author, to what do skeptics object regarding the commitment to disclose all information?

Caryn Tamber, "Proponents Love it, but Traditional Divorce Maryland Lawyers See Little Use for 'Collaborative Divorce'," *The Daily Record*, December 17, 2007. Reproduced by permission.

2. What concern do attorneys raise regarding relying on the opponent's word that he or she is telling the truth in collaborative divorce proceedings?
3. What might coerce a spouse with less money to agree to an unfair settlement in collaborative divorce proceedings?

Lawyers who handle collaborative divorce cases are passionate about the method.

They tout it as a kinder, gentler way to do divorce, a process that saves clients money and reduces the hostility between the soon-to-be exes.

Collaborative Divorce Not Necessary for Agreement

But some family law attorneys are, to put it mildly, unconvinced. They believe collaborative divorce is useful for the occasional couple but is, in general, a minefield of inflated hopes and potential ethical problems.

"I have no issue . . . with two lawyers sitting down with two clients to work out a deal, but why it's necessary to wrap all these conditions around it is beyond me," said David S. Goldberg, a Gaithersburg family law mediator.

In collaborative divorce, the spouses and their lawyers sign an agreement pledging to work out a settlement without litigation. There is no official discovery. There are no motions. There are no hearings.

If one party does take the case to court, both spouses must find new legal representation and new experts.

The two parties and their lawyers are often joined at the bargaining table by other professionals, such as mental health counselors and financial planners.

The idea of collaborative divorce is that the parties, having worked out financial and custody issues without contentious litigation, will be able to deal with each other respectfully in the future.

Suzy Eckstein of Oakley & Eckstein LLC in Rockville said that a pair of good divorce attorneys will almost always be able to reach a settlement and avoid litigation, even outside of a collaborative law context.

"Why not start there and save the parties a lot of heartache and money?" said Eckstein, who handles collaborative divorce.

The average collaborative divorce costs about $20,000 total, according to the International Academy of Collaborative Professionals. That contrasts with upward of $25,000 per side for a litigated divorce, according to Darcy A. Shoop, president of the Maryland Collaborative Practice Council.

Collaborative Divorce Not Best for Most

Shoop said collaborative divorce lets clients take a more active role in deciding the settlement terms, "which gives them a vested interest in how that outcome is achieved" and makes it more likely that agreements will be honored.

"They are not at the mercy of what lawyers are doing, what the judge is doing, what the custody evaluators are doing," said Shoop, of Rockville's Stein, Sperling, Bennett, De Jong, Driscoll & Greenfeig P.C.

People think collaborative lawyers and their clients "sit around and eat granola and sing Kumbaya," Shoop said. "No, no, no, these cases are hard. They take patience. They take skill. They take a whole skill set that I didn't really use in litigation."

Shoop conceded that some couples are not good candidates for collaborative divorce, including spouses with "serious domestic violence issues," mental illness or substance abuse problems. She said that, of the thirty-five collaborative divorces she has handled, the only two that did not succeed were those in which, midway through the process, a party proved to have mental health issues.

But, she said, between 85 percent and 90 percent of divorcing couples would benefit from handling their cases collaboratively.

That's far from the number Scott Strickler has in mind.

"Instead of it being good for 80 percent of cases, it's good for 20 percent of cases," the Bethesda divorce attorney said.

Full Disclosure Relies on Trust

Strickler, of Strickler, Sachitano & Hatfield P.A., said that people who have secrets are not good candidates for collaborative divorce, which emphasizes full disclosure of anything that could affect the settlement. That could be interpreted to favor disclosure of, for example, an affair, even if there is "nothing to be gained" by sharing the information, Strickler said.

Goldberg, the mediator, described collaborative divorce's preference for full disclosure more bluntly.

"That's Pollyanna crap, frankly," Goldberg said. "Nobody discloses everything; I don't care how pure everybody's motives are."

He said that even though clients undergoing collaborative divorce agree at the outset to fully disclose all assets and anything else relevant to the divorce settlement, it's "naive" to believe they understand all the implications of that promise.

He gave the hypothetical example of a client who, unbeknownst to her husband, has been having an affair and plans to marry her lover right after her divorce. She tells her lawyer that because she is getting remarried quickly, she does not care about getting alimony; she asks the lawyer to leverage the alimony so she can keep the house.

Goldberg said that if he were representing the woman in a non-collaborative case, he would do what she asked. In a collaborative case, however, he would be bound to disclose his client's intentions, he said.

Downsides to Collaborative Divorce

The primary downside to collaboration is that if it doesn't work, your collaborative lawyer is required to withdraw, and you have to start all over with a new lawyer and possibly new experts and advisers. This means a lot of expense and delay while you get your new lawyer up to speed and retain new professionals. . . .

In addition, some lawyers argue that collaborative law blurs the role of your attorney, who is expected to look for compromises and solutions acceptable to the other side while at the same time representing you and your interests. Of course, this criticism ignores the fact that if you have chosen to collaborate, *you* have decided that it is in your interests to find mutually acceptable solutions.

Another argument that can be made against collaboration as opposed to mediation is that because lawyers are more involved in the negotiating process than they generally are in mediation, you may be less likely to arrive at creative solutions—solutions that are outside what the law might prescribe (for example, trading payments for education or job-training now for a shorter period paying alimony in the future). . . . The more lawyers are involved in the process, the argument goes, the less outside-the-box thinking will be applied.

Finally, as in the case of an unsuccessful mediation, there is some risk that a case can become very adversarial if collaboration fails, since at that point there can be a tendency to give up on ever reaching a reasonable settlement.

Katherine E. Stoner, Divorce Without Court: A Guide to Mediation and Collaborative Divorce. *Berkeley, CA: Nolo, 2006.*

To the skeptics, the problem is not just that they would have to be absolutely truthful, even when doing so would hurt their clients' interests; it's that they would have to trust the other side to do the same.

Trust No Substitute for Discovery

"Can I just automatically assume since we're in collaborative law that everyone's telling the truth?" asked Harry Siegel, a solo practitioner in Columbia. "Is that a responsible way for an attorney to act?"

Siegel, who founded the family law section of the Maryland Trial Lawyers Association, said that in collaborative law, lawyers have "a much higher duty to the client to explain the potential negative consequences of collaborative law in terms of the honesty of the parties and the proceedings."

Joe Paradiso, a family lawyer with Paradiso, Taub, Sinay & Owel P.C. in Bethesda, echoed Siegel's concerns. Clients promise to disclose all of their assets, but there are no discovery tools in place to ensure that that happens, he said.

He and some of the other skeptics worried that a wily client looking to hide assets may choose collaborative divorce specifically because there is no formal discovery.

"There's no substitute for full investigations, signing documents under oath, independent investigation, depositions if necessary," Siegel said.

Attorneys Have Duties to Opposing Counsel

Eckstein said she believes collaborative divorce is actually a better method for making sure both sides are being truthful about their finances.

"In a litigation case, you have to ask questions in interrogatories in a stilted way, in deposition," she said. "People are always trying to hide the ball and duck the motion."

"If you're sitting in a room, you're all together, you have a neutral [financial expert] and you're looking the person in the eye, it's harder to lie," Eckstein said.

Those who remain unconvinced say they worry that malpractice complaints could follow collaborative divorce cases where an attorney relies on an opponent's word that he is telling the truth.

Strickler said he also has a problem with the part of the standard collaborative divorce agreement that requires each side to disclose the other's mistakes.

"In collaborative law, you're not allowed to take advantage of the mistakes of the other side," he complained.

For example, Strickler said, if opposing counsel does not realize that the settlement he has proposed will hurt his own client's income tax liability and help Strickler's, Strickler would be obligated to tell him.

Process Can Be Manipulated

The skeptics also expressed concern that the agreement to change attorneys and experts should the case go to court could coerce clients to settle—not because they want to and not because they are happy with the terms, but because they cannot afford to start from scratch.

That could be especially dangerous for the spouse with less money, Paradiso said.

"It creates this environment where one party can manipulate the process and effectively say, either play on my terms or we're history," Paradiso said. "It creates an environment where I think it could put an enormous amount of pressure on a financially dependent spouse."

Mediation Would Be as Good as Collaborative Divorce

The collaborative divorce skeptics believe that, although collaborative law may have some value, it's not so different from other divorce methods.

Siegel said that other ways of resolving divorce cases, such as court-backed alternative dispute resolution or private mediation, have room for the face-to-face discussions touted by backers of collaborative divorce.

"Anything that you can do inside the collaborative model you can do outside the collaborative model, but the reverse isn't true," Siegel said. "If you're inside the collaborative model, your hands are tied on those issues of honesty and continuation of representation if it doesn't work."

And Paradiso said that the couple who can successfully complete collaborative divorce, those whose relationship is sufficiently cordial to permit a low-key, non-litigious approach, would probably be able to use any method of divorce.

"I would argue that the type of client who is well-suited for collaborative law could do the same exact thing in mediation," Paradiso said. "If you get that 10 percent, 15 percent, 20 percent of people who can really work through their issues, they're doing that anyway."

Settlement Negotiations Already Are Collaborative

Paradiso also said he is tired of collaborative law proponents discounting his opposition to the practice because he has not gone through collaborative training—a two- or three-day session sponsored by one of several collaborative law societies.

"It's as if you haven't yet found God and if you take the course, you'll know," Paradiso said.

The Maryland Collaborative Practice Council keeps track of people who have been collaboratively trained here, and according to Shoop, the current tally is almost 400. Most are lawyers, though some are financial or mental health professionals.

Siegel said he has never taken collaborative law training—and that he doesn't have to.

"I do 'collaborative law' every day," Siegel said. "I don't need to have the moniker of a formal organization, but the essence of collaborative law is finding a way, if you can, to meet your clients' goals . . . without having to resort to rolling the dice in court.

"More than often it works. Sometimes it doesn't work," he said. "Sometimes even people in good faith have to go to court on initial issues to understand that the alternative of court is perhaps not the best model for them."

Viewpoint 3

"Facing decades of good years ahead of them, financially healthy and not constrained by the stigma of divorce that kept many of their mothers married, [women] make the leap."

Divorce Provides a Fresh Start for Women

Gail Rosenblum

Gail Rosenblum argues in the following viewpoint that divorce can provide a fresh start for women who are bored or unhappy with their marriage. Men, she says, don't see it coming, though women say they signal their unhappiness years before the divorce. The author contends that women, financially healthy and no longer bound by the stigma of divorce, are not satisfied with mediocre marriages. Rosenblum writes for the Star Tribune.

As you read, consider the following questions:

1. According to a survey cited by the author, how long had one-third of women fifty years old or older been thinking about leaving before doing so?
2. According to a worldwide study of divorce cited by the author, which gender most often instigates divorce?

Gail Rosenblum, "A Different Divorce; Women Who Walk," *Star Tribune*, April 2, 2007.

3. According to that same worldwide study, what was the biggest reason for divorce?

Alicia Lahti knew that people viewed her 23-year marriage as happy. And why not? Her husband was "a wonderful man," she said. Together they built a home and careers, traveled and raised two "brilliant kids," now 17 and 21. So relatives and friends were shocked when, a year and a half ago, 46-year-old Lahti asked for a divorce. "I loved my husband, but I was not in love with him like you should be in love," said Lahti of St. Louis Park. "It was very hard to tell him. Society teaches us to be a good mother, good wife, to stay together for the sake of the children. But it's OK to move forward."

Men Don't See It Coming

A growing number of women seem to be drawing the same conclusion. Although the first-time divorce rate has been declining since the 1970s, and now hovers just under 50 percent, there's been an unmistakable increase in the percentage of midlife women like Lahti doing the asking. A study commissioned by AARP [American Association of Retired Persons] in 2004 revealed that nationwide, women in their 40s, 50s and beyond now initiate 66 percent of divorces. More than one-fourth of their husbands, the study reported, were stupefied. Never saw it coming.

"I am a divorced father who was simply dropped by his wife," e-mailed Curtis from St. Paul, who asked that his full name not be used to protect his children. His "past" wife, as he calls her, has moved away and he does not keep in touch with her. "There was no drug, alcohol, infidelity or abuse reasons. She simply said that I was 'boring' and 'spent too much time with the kids.' This is the most common scenario in the majority of divorces. It's not neat and clean like pro-divorce people want to make it out to be."

Be True to Yourself

While "boring" may make some wince, it's not far from the reasons many women give for leaving. Physical and emotional abuse, infidelity and substance abuse are still high on the list, but women more often speak about simple unhappiness, lousy communication and loneliness.

Facing decades of good years ahead of them, financially healthy and not constrained by the stigma of divorce that kept many of their mothers married, they make the leap.

A year ago, Karol Thompson, 58, called a divorce lawyer after "hanging in there" for 16 years of power struggles and difficult stepfamily dynamics. "Inside, you still care about what people think, but you have to be true to yourself," said Thompson, a Minneapolis mother of two grown children. The decision was not easy. She's living off credit cards, she said, and looking forward to getting on track financially. She's moved from a beautiful lake home with gardens and loons to a small apartment. Sometimes she fears what the future holds for a woman nearing 60. But she feels that she did the right thing. She is reconnecting with girlfriends, attending plays, learning photography and doting on her grandson. "I'm just trying to get those voices out of my head," she said, "and enjoy the quietude."

Marriage Not Good Enough for Women

While many men are blindsided by their wives' departure, many women say they sent out signals for years. In the AARP study, about one-third of women 50 and older said they began thinking about leaving at least two years before they did it. One in ten women thought about it for a decade or longer. "I never talked to people about issues in my marriage," Lahti said. "I held everything in. That was terribly wrong."

The problem may be in how women send signals, said Neil Chethik, author of the new book, *VoiceMale*, featuring men's candid opinions about marriage, sex and housework.

Women Find Divorce Liberating

Women are far more likely than men to come out of divorce feeling liberated, relieved and happy, a study has shown.

Rather than feeling devastated at the end of their marriage, women are more likely to see the split as a fresh start, but their former husbands remain stressed and unhappy even years after they receive their decree absolute.

Maxine Frith, "Women Happier than Men After Divorce, Study Shows," The Independent, *July 4, 2005.*

Women like to talk it out, he said, which is difficult for many men who are not as well-trained in the face-to-face emotional approach. "Men resist and resist and then the woman stops pushing it. Frankly, that's when I say to men, 'Watch out.' When she turns off, it's not that she's forgotten. It's that she's started to give up on the relationship."

One reality for men, Chethik discovered in his research, is that marriage is often good enough for them. "But women feel like, if it's not very good and growing and getting better, it's not good enough."

Still, not all divorces are initiated enthusiastically. Some women, particularly in high-income couplings, may feel pushed to petition for the split, to take back control after a husband announces he is leaving her for someone else. Deirdre Bair, author of *Calling it Quits: Late-Life Divorce and Starting Over*, calls this "CEO-itis: If he's going to ditch me, I'm going in there to get mine first." That doesn't mean that these women aren't devastated. Aside from the emotional toll, some older women have never balanced a checkbook. Kent Peterson, a certified divorce financial analyst in Waverly, Minn., said that 90 percent of his clients seeking financial advice prior to divorce are women. "Most are over 40 because, at that point, they have significant assets to protect and divide. Once they understand how this can be OK, they feel they can move ahead with confidence," he said.

Women Leaving Men Worldwide

Bair's research, which included interviews with 184 women and 126 men from their early 50s to 80s, supports the finding that women are generally the instigators, and not just in the United States. "All of a sudden, it's women in record numbers all over the world," Bair said, including Australia, New Zealand and Switzerland. In Germany, "it's an epidemic." The biggest reason, she said, is "emotional distance. [Women] said, 'We just didn't have anything in common; he never showed me any affection, or a compliment or a birthday present.' They just didn't want to be a part of that relationship anymore."

Men leave for many of the same reasons, she said. They fall out of love or into love with someone else. They're tired of doing what others expect of them. Not all make the dramatic leap to divorce. Bair said she was stunned by the number of couples in her research she calls "divorced while married." These couples, she said, "live separate lives within the same house. They eat meals separately and have separate bedrooms. They have separate friends and separate activities but, when the kids come home or company comes in, they pretend they're together and everything is just fine."

While women who do walk sing the praises of freedom, many men left in the lurch quickly get down to the business of recoupling. In the AARP study, more than 80 percent of men in their 50s had a serious, exclusive relationship as quickly as two years post-divorce. (And despite their cry for freedom, 75 percent of women did, too.)

Lahti and her former husband (who politely declined to be interviewed) divorced using the more amicable approach of collaborative law. The process was completed in under two months. After a year of "learning to love myself and becoming whole again," Lahti said, she's slowly getting back into dating.

Even though it was a "respectful divorce," Lahti said it wasn't easy on anybody in the family. Her son lives with her, but he sees his dad whenever he wants. "If he wants to be with his dad on Christmas, I say, 'Go. Have a good day.' In the long run, it's a blessing for everyone," Lahti said. "I sure hope that, if [my children] are in a relationship or marriage that is not loving and joyful, they will have the courage to move on in a respectful way."

VIEWPOINT 4

> *"Mediation is the best legal option for terminating the marriage, while keeping the process focused on the needs of the children."*

Mediated Divorce Is Best for Children

Darcia C. Tudor

Darcia C. Tudor argues in the following viewpoint that a "good" (nonadversarial) divorce achieved through mediation is best for children. She says adversarial divorce does not work because it costs too much financially and emotionally. Cooperation, she argues, makes it easier to change from a nuclear to a binuclear home. Parents with mediated agreements, she contends, report less parental conflict. Tudor is an attorney, mediator, and clinical therapist.

As you read, consider the following questions:

1. In the author's view, what negative effect does adversarial divorce have on legal and therapeutic professionals involved?
2. Who, in the author's view, are the only true experts on what is best for a family?

Darcia C. Tudor, "The 'Good Divorce' is a Necessity for Families With Children," divorcenet.com, December 18, 2007. Reproduced by permission of the author.

3. According to research cited by the author, what percentage of parents reached an agreement through mediation?

The United States has the highest rate of divorce in the industrialized world. It is estimated that 25% of the adults in this country between the ages of 18 and 44 are the products of divorced households. While some children exhibit no ill effects, studies have shown them to be at an increased risk of experiencing academic and social problems. The risks continue in adolescence with ". . . parental divorce and its associated stressors [being] associated with increased probability of teenage pregnancy, school dropout, and adult mental health problems."

In this country, the stigma related to divorce has waned over the years. Most people believe, however, that children who share the experience of the ending of a marriage will suffer some degree of psychological harm, developmental setback, or the loss of a meaningful relationship with one parent. In the past, the focus has been on the "event": the divorce. Researchers and theorists have recently advocated a change in our focus. [Researchers] Farlene, Wolchik & Karoly, 1988 reasoned that, despite the increased likelihood of maladjustment after a divorce, the majority of children raised in separate households adjusted well and did not exhibit problematic behaviors.

Divorce, like the unexpected death of a parent, the onset of a life-threatening illness of a child, or the unsuspecting loss of the primary earner's employment, creates a temporal family crisis that places an extraordinary amount of psychological, financial, and physical stress on each member of the family. Notwithstanding, it is how the family adapts to the crisis and transitions into the future that makes the difference for a well adjusted or poorly adjusted child. How the family reorganizes, not the fact that an unpredicted life event required change within its structure, will determine the emotional and economic "fate" of the children. Parents who want to minimize the potential for a harmful transition from a nuclear to a binuclear family will choose the course of the "Good" Divorce.

Cooperation Minimizes Harm from Divorce

A "Good" Divorce allows the intimate personal relationship between the parents to end, while sanctioning the children's continuing intimacy with both parents and permitting them to maintain a relationship with both parents and their extended families. A "Bad" Divorce enmeshes the children in marital conflicts during the transition, undermines the children's relationship with the other parent and his or her extended family, and places the children in an impoverished or uncertain financial situation at its legal conclusion.

The adversarial process of dissolving a marriage encourages legal and therapeutic professionals to take sides in the battle over the culturally esteemed derivatives of the relationship: the children and the assets. All too often, the mother's source of power in the conflict lies in her influence over the children and the father's in his control over the assets. Parents today know that the adversarial process does not work. It costs too much financially and emotionally. Yet, they are seduced by their anger, led by their grief, inspired by their fear, and in need of a success in the face of their feelings of personal failure. Parents today need to be encouraged to realize it is a conscious, but unreasonable, choice to participate in the process of a "Bad" Divorce. The "Good" Divorce is the only logical choice once one realizes that it does, and will, minimize the detrimental effects of divorce. Parents who chose compromise for the sake of the children and cooperation in the face of frustration reap the rewards of a continuing, but separate, household with a family and children who weathered the inevitable storms of divorce.

Cooperation Helps Children and Parents Adapt

The dissolution of the parents' relationship involves a long process for children to adapt to extensive familial reorganization and environmental changes, while in the midst of their own personal development. They must reconstruct their social networks, redefine family relationships, and re-establish a household by forming a "binuclear" home. While addressing these external changes, they must also adapt intra-psychically. They must acknowledge the reality of the separation, deal with their feelings of loss and rejection, acknowledge their anger, forgive their parents, accept the permanence of the divorce, and achieve realistic hope for future loving relationships.

Parents who opt for the "Bad" Divorce adapt to the stressors created during the transition in maladaptive ways, such as conflict, substance abuse, isolation, or avoidance, creating a developmentally hostile environment for their children. Research clearly establishes that parents who choose the path of the "Good" Divorce have the opportunity to adapt positively to the transformation from a "nuclear" to a "binuclear" home and are more likely to have financial support and subsequent security and stability, which generally can only be provided through cooperative post-dissolution parenting arrangements.

Parents with the courage and insight to choose the positive alternative, or the "Good" Divorce, must change the way they "think" about divorce. One out of every two marriages is dissolved. Therefore, parental separation has become the norm, not an abnormal shameful event. A divorce, like a marriage, is not defined in a single day, but is a series of events: a conversion from the emotional, financial, and spiritual unity of a single household to equally loving and financially secure binuclear households. The relationship between parent and child does not have to end, unless the unspoken, or spoken, family rules require the children to terminate the relationship with one to preserve the relationship with the other. Parents who participate in the "Good" Divorce change their behavior towards the other spouse and the traditional cultural rules that prohibit cooperative and positive interaction between former lovers.

Mediation Lets You Decide What's Best

One of the great features of mediation is that you and your spouse get to decide what's best for you, even if it's different from what the laws provide. There are a few things you cannot legally agree to—such as giving up the right to receive child support—but these are rare. Other than the few exceptions, you are free to make whatever agreement is best for you.

Katherine E. Stoner,
Divorce Without Court:
A Guide to Mediation and Collaborative Divorce.
Berkeley, CA: Nolo, 2006.

A divorce can simply redefine the context in which a family lives, or it can be an excuse for the termination of the intimate psychological and supportive connections between its members. If keeping the family a "family" for the sake of the children is the number one parental priority, all out "war" is not an option because it is certain to hinder, or destroy, the children's ability to maintain a relationship with both parents.

"Good" Divorce Can Minimize Harm to Children

Parents who choose the path of the "Good" Divorce manage their own divorce, and make their own decisions after appropriate advice and counsel. They realize that they are the only true experts on what is best for their family. They seek guidance and direction in order to make informed decisions without relinquishing their control over the process or their responsibility for the actions of their legal representatives and family agents.

In order to minimize the negative affects on their children, astute and conscientious parents:

- Slow down the process to allow their children to adjust to the changes
- Accept their children's needs and rights to have relationships with both parents
- Cooperate with their "ex" if only for the sake of the children
- Establish a limited parenting partnership with clear rules which encourage a positive vision of a new "bi-nuclear" family
- Permit the expansion of their children's family to include non-biological kin
- Find new ways of relating independently with their children

In addition, parents must integrate their past relationship, and subsequent divorce, into their own lives in a healthy way. They need to:

- Remember the good parts of the relationship within the context of the family before the divorce and share those memories with their children
- Face their losses without drowning in the pain
- Forgive themselves and their ex
- Let go of their anger

Mediation Is Best Method for "Good" Divorce

Last, but not least, parents who choose the course of the "Good" Divorce must select a process for ending the relationship which is conducive to these goals. The adversarial process is guaranteed not to promote the cooperation, communication, and compliant behaviors that are necessary for parents to co-parent after they cease to be spouses. The adversarial process increases stressors for children because it often enhances the level of parental conflict and raises uncertainties about future contact with both parents. Mediation is the best legal option for terminating the marriage, while keeping the process focused on the needs of the children.

[Researchers] Emery, Laumann-Billings, Walron, Sbarra, and Dillon (2001) conducted a study on the relationship between parental conflict and alternative methods of dispute resolution. The results of their study confirmed that most parents reached an agreement through mediation (89%), drastically reducing the litigation, and that the agreements were more likely to provide for joint legal custody, while maintaining the tradition of the mother as the primary parent. Those who mediated their agreements tended to report less parental conflict and reported more child-related discussions with the nonresidential parent. The process tends to open the door to "child-centered" communication and change.

Mediation Enhances Psychological Adjustment of Children

The results did suggest a correlation between mediation and enhanced post-divorce psychological adjustment of the children. Nonresidential parents who mediated reported significantly more involvement with their children, tended to have more telephone contact, visit more frequently, and be more involved in making decisions involving their children. Despite the fact that lessened parental conflict was not associated with the method of dispute resolution, this study offers strong proof that mediation results in the non-primary residential parent having a higher level of contact and involvement with his or her children after divorce.

The "Good" Divorce is the only viable option for parents who do not want to waste their financial resources and emotional energy in an attempt to gain assets or the hearts of their children when they can only be won through a quiet, consistent, and sharing love. The "Good" Divorce is the logical and compassionate choice for loving parents who face the unexpected life transition of ending a marriage.

Periodical Bibliography

The following articles have been selected to supplement the diverse views presented in this chapter.

Nicola Berkovic	"Children to Receive Help and a Voice in Their Parents' Break-up," *The Australian*, March 22, 2008.
Carolyn Pape Cowan, Philip A. Cowan, Marsha Kline Pruett, and Kyle Pruett	"An Approach to Preventing Coparenting Conflict and Divorce in Low-Income Families," *Family Process*, March 1, 2007.
David Crary	"Some Couples Find a Less Contentious Route to Divorce," *The Washington Post*, December 23, 2007.
Kira Goldenberg	"A Personal Divorce Trainer: Breakups Can Go Better When Coaches' Advice Smoothes the Process," *The Hartford Courant*, June 23, 2007.
Melissa Harris	"Same Split with a Lot Less Spat: Howard Teams Guide Collaborative Divorce," *The Baltimore Sun*, October 5, 2007.
Elana Katz	"A Family Therapy Perspective on Mediation," *Family Process*, vol. 46, no. 1, March 2007.
Weimin Mo	"The Divorce Culture and Picture Books for Young Children," *International Journal of Early Childhood*, January 1, 2007.
Alison Roberts	"Split Divorce: 'Collaborative Divorce' Helps People Avoid Judges, Confrontation and Drama," *Sacramento Bee*, January 14, 2007.
Jennifer Torres	"Divorce Without the Ugly Court Battle," *The Record* (Stockton, CA), September 24, 2007.
Nicola Walker	"Divorce Doesn't Have To Be Hell on Earth," *Birmingham Post*, June 18, 2008.
Ann Weber	"Getting Along with Your Ex: Children Are Hurt When Divorced Parents Duel," *The Blade* (OH), February 17, 2008.

For Further Discussion

Chapter 1

1. Michelle Bryant argues that divorce harms children, but Donna Olmstead contends that children can adapt to divorce. Do the authors differ in how they define "harm" to children of divorce?
2. Jay Zagorsky argues that divorce causes poverty. Can you tell whether the same factors that cause divorce are responsible for differences in wealth accumulation or whether divorce alone accounts for the differences? Does it matter and, if so, why?

Chapter 2

1. Katherine Shaw Spaht argues that covenant marriage can reduce divorce, but Don Monkerud argues that covenant marriage does not appeal to most people. What values make covenant marriage appeal to some but not to others, and how, if at all, do such values relate to the likelihood of divorce?
2. Ailee Slater argues that reducing poverty will reduce divorce. What data does she cite in support of her argument? What other data would you like to see to be fully convinced of the merits of her view?
3. Amanda Cable argues that the Surrendered Wives movement can save marriages, but Ceri Radford believes that the movement demeans women. To what values and outcomes does each author give importance and how might that affect the viewpoints of each?

Chapter 3

1. Stephen Baskerville argues that no-fault divorce is harmful to society, but Nahal Toosi contends that fault should not be required for divorce. How do the authors differ, if at all, in assigning importance to personal happiness compared to preservation of the marriage?
2. Marilyn Gardner favors joint physical custody of children, but Eleanor Bailey holds the practice in disfavor. Do you think the fact that mothers are more likely than fathers to receive sole custody of children influences the viewpoint of either author? Why or why not?

Chapter 4

1. Collaborative divorce involves the expense of employing not only attorneys, but also psychologists and financial advisors; however, some people who divorce can barely afford the filing fees and the attorney fees. How do you think the authors of each viewpoint would feel about public funding of collaborative divorce?
2. Darcia C. Tudor argues that mediated divorce is best when children are involved. Compare her viewpoint with the viewpoints concerning collaborative divorce, and explain the differences between mediated divorce and collaborative divorce.

Organizations to Contact

The editors have compiled the following list of organizations concerned with the issues debated in this book. The descriptions are derived from materials provided by the organizations. All have publications or information available for interested readers. The list was compiled on the date of publication of the present volume; the information provided here may change. Be aware that many organizations take several weeks or longer to respond to inquiries, so allow as much time as possible.

American Academy of Matrimonial Lawyers (AAML)
150 N. Michigan Ave., Ste. 2040, Chicago, IL 60601
(312) 263-6477 • Fax: (312) 263-7682
E-mail: office@aaml.org
Web site: www.aaml.org

The mission of the American Academy of Matrimonial Lawyers (AAML) is to encourage the study, improve the practice, elevate the standards, and advance the cause of matrimonial law to help protect the welfare of the family and society. AAML has chapters throughout the United States and in other countries and can provide referrals to attorneys specializing in matrimonial and family law. The organization's Web site has articles, news, and information on legal issues related to divorce.

American Coalition for Fathers and Children
1718 M St. NW, #187, Washington, DC 20036
(800) 978-3237 • Fax: (703) 442-5313
E-mail: info@acfc.org
Web site: www.acfc.org

The American Coalition for Fathers and Children advocates the creation of a family law system, a legislative system, and public awareness that promote equal rights for fathers affected by divorce, the breakup of a family, or the establishment of paternity. The organization's Web site has articles and information about divorce of special interest to fathers.

Association for Children for Enforcement of Support (ACES)
3474 Raymont Blvd., 2nd Floor
University Heights, OH 44118
(800) 738-2237
Web site: www.childsupport-aces.org

The Association for Children for Enforcement of Support (ACES) is a self-help, nonprofit, child-support organization that teaches custodial parents what they need to do to collect child support. ACES has 350 chapters across the United States. The organization's Web site has news concerning child support collection issues.

Association of Family and Conciliation Courts
6525 Grand Teton Plz., Madison, WI 53719
(608) 664-3750 • Fax: (608) 664-3751
E-mail: afcc@afccnet.org
Web site: www.afccnet.org

The Association of Family and Conciliation Courts is an international association of judges, lawyers, counselors, custody evaluators, and mediators. The organization maintains a library of videos, pamphlets, and other publications on custody and visitation issues, child support, mediation, and more. This group also sponsors parent education programs and conferences on a wide range of child welfare issues.

Children's Rights Council (CRC)
8181 Professional Pl., Ste. 240, Landover, MD 20785
(301) 459-1220
E-mail: info@crckids.org
Web site: www.crckids.org

The Children's Rights Council (CRC) is a national, nonprofit organization dedicated to assisting children of separation and divorce through advocacy and parenting education. CRC works to assure a child the frequent, meaningful, and continuing contact with two parents and extended family that the child would normally have during a marriage. CRC works to strengthen families through education, favoring family formation and family preservation. The organization's searchable Web site has news and information on divorce issues as they affect children.

The Coalition for Collaborative Divorce
PMB 623, Calabasas, CA 91302-1502
(800) 559-3724
E-mail: info@nocourtdivorce.com
Web site: www.nocourtdivorce.com

The Coalition for Collaborative Divorce provides collaborative divorce services in southern California, but also has articles and information about the collaborative divorce process in general.

Covenant Marriage Movement
PO Box 780, Forest, VA 24551
(800) 311-1662 • Fax: (434) 525-9480
E-mail: info@covenantmarriage.com
Web site: www.covenantmarriage.com

The Covenant Marriage Movement is an organization that exists to promote the covenant marriage movement. The Web site has articles about covenant marriage, news about covenant marriage legislation, and events related to covenant marriage.

Divorce Care
PO Box 1739, Wake Forest, NC 27588
(800) 489-7778
E-mail: info@divorcecare.org
Web site: www.divorcecare.com

Divorce Care provides resources to help divorced people heal from the experience. Local chapters provide support groups and seminars. The organization also sells books, videos, and CDs on topics related to adjusting to divorce.

Institute for American Values
1841 Broadway, Ste. 211, New York, NY 10023
(212) 246-3942 • Fax: (212) 541-6665
E-mail: info@americanvalues.org
Web site: www.americanvalues.org

The Institute for American Values Web site has many articles and reports about divorce and its effect on children. The institute promotes traditional family roles. The organization's Web site also links to research resources at the Center for Marriage and Families.

Parents Without Partners (PWP)
1650 S. Dixie Hwy., Ste. 510, Boca Raton, FL 33432
(800) 637-7974
Web site: www.parentswithoutpartners.org

Parents Without Partners (PWP) provides single parents and their children with an opportunity for enhancing personal growth, self-confidence, and sensitivity toward others by offering an environment for support, friendship, and the exchange of parenting techniques. For the minor children of single parents, PWP offers the opportunity to meet peers who are thriving within the same family structure. Services are provided through local chapters, which also can provide resources on child support and custody issues for both custodial and noncustodial parents.

The Vanier Institute of the Family
94 Centrepointe Dr., Ottawa, Ontario K2G 6B1
Canada
(613) 228-8500 • Fax: (613) 228-8007
E-mail: webmaster@vifamily.ca
Web site: www.vifamily.ca

The Vanier Institute of the Family's mission is to create awareness of, and to provide leadership on, the importance and strengths of families in Canada and the challenges they face in their structural, demographic, economic, cultural, and social diversity. The organization's searchable database provides access to news, commentary, and research concerning many divorce issues.

Bibliography of Books

Kirstin Armstrong	*Happily Ever After: Walking with Peace and Courage Through a Year of Divorce*, New York: Faith Words, 2007.
Cheri Arterburn	*The Perfect Divorce*, San Diego, CA: B & C Publishing, 2005.
Nadir Baksh and Laurie Murphy	*In the Best Interest of the Child: A Manual for Divorcing Parents*, Prescott, AZ: Hohm Press, 2007.
Dierdre Blair	*Calling It Quits: Late-Life Divorce and Starting Over*, New York: Random House, 2007.
Michelle Borquez, Connie Wetzel, Rosalind Spinks-Seay, and Carla Sue Nelson	*Live, Laugh, Love Again: A Christian Woman's Survival Guide to Divorce*, New York: Warner Faith, 2006.
Gary D. Chapman	*Covenant Marriage: Building Communication & Intimacy*, Nashville: Broadman and Holman Publishers, 2003.
Alison Clarke-Stewart and Cornelia Brentano	*Divorce: Causes and Consequences*, New Haven, CT: Yale University Press, 2006.
Emily Doskow	*Nolo's Essential Guide for Divorce*, Berkeley, CA: Nolo, 2006.

Emily M. Douglas	*Mending Broken Families: Social Policies for Divorced Families: How Effective Are They?* Lanham, MD: Rowman & Littlefield Publishers, 2006.
Jay Folberg, Ann L. Milne, and Peter Salem, eds.	*Divorce and Family Mediation: Models, Techniques, and Applications*, New York: Guilford Press, 2004.
Debbie Ford	*Spiritual Divorce: Divorce as a Catalyst for an Extraordinary Life*, New York: HarperCollins, 2006.
Harold Fuess	*Divorce in Japan: Family, Gender and the State*, Stanford, CA: Stanford University Press, 2004.
Wendy Jaffe	*The Divorce Lawyers' Guide to Staying Married*, Los Angeles: Volt Press, 2006.
Mark J. Kittleson	*The Truth About Divorce*, New York: Book Builders LLC, 2005.
Sam Margulies	*Man's Guide to a Civilized Divorce: How to Divorce with Grace, a Little Class, and a Lot of Common Sense*, Emmaus, PA: Rodale, 2004.
Elizabeth Marquardt	*Between Two Worlds: The Inner Lives of Children of Divorce*, New York: Crown, 2005.
Elizabeth Marquardt	*We're Still Family: What Grown Children Have to Say About Their Parents' Divorce*, New York: HarperCollins, 2005.

Deborah Moskovitch	*The Smart Divorce: Proven Strategies and Valuable Advice from 100 Top Divorce Lawyers, Financial Advisers, Counselors, and Other Experts*, Chicago: Chicago Review Press, 2007.
Laurie Perry	*Drunk, Divorced and Covered in Cat Hair*, Deerfield Beach, FL: Health Communications, 2007.
Yossef Rapoport	*Marriage, Money and Divorce in Medieval Islamic Society*, Cambridge: Cambridge University Press, 2005.
Daniel Sitarz	*Divorce Yourself*, Carbondale, IL: Nova Publishing Company, 2005.
Katherine E. Stoner	*Divorce Without Court: A Guide to Mediation and Collaborative Divorce*, Santa Cruz, CA: Nolo Press, 2005.
John Trent	*Breaking the Cycle of Divorce*, Carol Stream, IL: Tyndale House Publishers, 2006.
Trudi Strain Trueit	*Surviving Divorce: Teens Talk About What Hurts and What Helps*, New York: Scholastic, 2007.
Stuart G. Webb and Ronald D. Ousky	*The Collaborative Way to Divorce*, New York: Hudson Street Press, 2006.
Violet Woodhouse	*Divorce and Money: How to Make the Best Financial Decisions During Divorce*, Santa Cruz, CA: Nolo Press, 2007.

Index

C

D

E

F

G

W

Y

Z